DON'T BE A WIMP

RAISE A

STRONG LEADER

PARENTING STRATEGIES FROM
CONCEPTION TO LATE ADULTHOOD

D1605560

By Dr. Henry J. Svec

ISBN: 978-0-9684275-0-7

Publisher
Etrack Inc.
801 Talbot St.
London Ontario Canada
N6A 2V7

Editor: Alethea Spiridon
Formatting by Indie Publishing Group
www.indiepublishinggroup.com

Contents

1 Introduction 1

2 What does it mean to "Parent with Courage?" . . . 9

3 What is the Makeup of a Strong Leader? 13

4 How to Use this Book. 21

5 Claude Riopelle. 23

6 Gary Waterman 39

7 Ho Tek 57

8 Kimberly Joines 71

9 John Milne 107

10 Natasha Borota 127

11 Parenting and Blueberry Pie 157

12 Stages of Child and Parental Development Today 159

13 The Six Strategies to Parent with Courage, But Wait a Minute, this isn't Rocket Science. 165

14 Your Action Plan. 173

15 Are you a wimp, or do you Parent with Courage? 177

Appendix 1 181

Conclusion 193

Endnotes .195

1

Introduction

THIS BOOK HAS been brewing inside me for a long time.

For the past twenty-six years I've tried to help over twelve thousand people in my clinics. With that, I've listened to and talked with many teachers who tell me that children today are different. A coach tells me that when he tells a player to get in the game, the high school student refuses, saying the game is out of reach and he would rather not play. Teachers also tell me it takes months to train young children in the early grades how to be respectful and understand that "no means no," that many of the children in their classrooms, regardless of how young, will use cell phones while the teachers are trying to teach. I am told that some teachers must allow children to use their phones during exams, and that students text answers to each other.

I was sitting on the train a few years ago, and the talk quickly turned to what we did for a living and the state of the world. The gentleman sitting beside me told the story of why he was taking "early" retirement from his job as a professor in the faculty of medicine at a prominent university. He said he was sick of it. Each year he would get calls from parents telling him why he couldn't fail their child because they didn't show up for class or hand in a lab or assignment. When he would refuse their request, he would get called into the dean's office and be told to fix the problem.

Later, I spoke with a group of educational counselors at a local university who told me that students with ADHD would often swamp their offices in the days *after* an assignment, paper, or exam was due. I questioned their position, wondering why it mattered as they would get a zero for not meeting the deadline. "No one fails today," they said. "We just help them get something in before the end of the year."

Some years ago, after interviewing a group of candidates for a job at one of our clinics, I received a call from the parent of one of the candidates suggesting that the salary and benefits we were offering weren't enough for their "baby." Well, we hadn't made a choice yet or indicated any details as the position had not been filled, but we were clear he wasn't our choice.

This next example further explains the severity of the problem in our society today.

Recently in Texas, a teen was determined not responsible for killing four people while driving intoxicated because "…psychologist called by the defence_testified that the teenager had affluenza, indicating his behavioural problems were influenced by a troubled upbringing in a wealthy family where privilege prevented him from grasping the consequences of his actions." In short, as reported in *The Guardian*, being spoiled by his parents lead to his behaviour. Forget for a moment that "affluenza" is a made up diagnosis not recognized by any professional organization. Consider the fact that the teen inflicted with affluenza recently violated his probation order when his mother reportedly took him to Mexico after he was seen on social media intoxicated, a violation of his probation conditions. Mom continued to support her son's criminal behaviour by not giving him the opportunity to face the consequences of his actions. She was parenting as a Wimp rather than with Courage.

As I started thinking a great deal about some of the behaviour others and I were witnessing, it became clear to me that parents want to do what is best for their children, but many don't know what that is or looks like. Parenting is a confusing profession today. We all want to raise and mentor children to become strong leaders, to be confident, lead their families, lead in business, lead in their communities, and be true to what is right and just. But no one has told us anything about how to parent children to help them *develop* those leadership skills. This book will help you do that.

Parents are told that any form of discipline or punishment is a bad thing. They are told that their job is to make sure their child never experiences pain or the need for anything. That children have the right to make decisions even as young as eight years old, decisions that may be lifesaving, but theirs to make nevertheless. Parents consent to anything and everything a child wants. Parents who do this are parenting as wimps, not Parenting with Courage. We've forgotten that the job of parenting is to make sure that when you leave this planet your child is able to survive and thrive without you.

We've forgotten that the strategies you use as a parent shouldn't be those that make *you* feel good or happy. Just as sixty is the new forty or fifty, being eighteen may be the new twelve. Childhood has seemed to extend well beyond a child's eighteenth birthday. Parents are being asked to support their children emotionally and psychologically until their child is well into their thirties.

But what does that mean? In the pages that follow, I will provide you with strategies and solutions to help you understand and work with your children as they move through middle age.

Grandparents, aunts, and uncles are being co-opted into helping with the parenting task as well. Some years ago when I wrote my first ebook, I said that grandparents only had one job. Their job was to spoil the child, break all the rules, and then send them back home to mom and dad. Not anymore. Extended family members are needed to help in the current parenting crisis like never before.

Parenting techniques to help raise a strong leader, a child who becomes a responsible, hardworking, true-to-their-beliefs citizen have not been easily explained or understood. I wrote this book to help you with that.

I decided to seek out those around me and beyond, to speak with those strong leaders, and find out how they were parented. I picked a group of six—two were close friends, two others that I had known briefly, and two strangers—to help me find out what their experience of being parented was like growing up. I wanted to find out if there were common parenting experiences that they encountered.

For this book I interviewed an Olympian who has won over forty international medals for skiing while strapped to a sit-ski after breaking her back at the age of eighteen. I also had the opportunity to interview her mother and grandmother to further explore how they parented their daughter. I interviewed a thirty-year-old entrepreneur from Waterloo, Ontario, who has created a multimillion dollar service business

I interviewed two educators who are close friends, both leading in sports at the University of Western Ontario, winning three National Championships in football, but then leading as educators and each uniquely with their families and social networks. One chose to put his life on hold for eighteen years to raise his three daughters, the other making a life-changing decision after a health scare.

I interviewed one of only two African American head

football coaches in Canada who demonstrated incredible leadership when a tragedy struck his home community.

I interviewed a woman in her forties who has built up a private company and dedicates her time to charity work, a woman who demonstrates strong leadership by example to other young aspiring entrepreneurs.

I tried to find through these interviews a common thread of types of parenting styles they experienced that contributed to their becoming a strong leader. You will read how I then took those experiences of the strong leaders and combined them with my professional background, experience, and training to help you Parent with Courage. The six strategies I created are required if you want to do all you can to raise your child well.

You will learn that a specific type of discipline is necessary to raise a strong leader because without discipline in the home, the child has little chance of developing self-discipline as an adult. You will learn the different ways to say no to your child and why they matter. You will begin to model specific behaviour yourself because everything you do or say, your child sees and soaks in. You can't just say what you want them to do; you have to model it. You will also learn about the power of the environment after conception. It's an area we don't know a lot about yet, but are starting to explore and discuss.

You will also consider why the majority of the leaders in this book were spanked as children. Now before you close the cover and stop reading because you are disgusted with the thought that I will be telling you to do this, remember that close to seventy percent of adults feel that occasionally spanking a child above the age of two and below the age of thirteen is permissible. In Canada, the Supreme Court has continued to extend that permission to parents, and even teachers, to help correct child behaviour. We have to talk about spanking in this book because no one else seems to want to. It is legal, permissible, and, in some cases, required.

I have a number of people to thank for this book. The six leaders interviewed gave up their valuable time, revealing information about themselves that, at times, caused significant emotional pain, information that has never been discussed in public before. I thank them for their courage in trusting me to tell their story with honesty and grace with the sole purpose of helping millions of parents understand how to Parent with Courage to develop our next generation of strong leaders.

2

What does it mean to "Parent with Courage?"

WHEN YOU SIGNED up to be a parent and your child was conceived, you likely were excited. For many reasons, this now represents a change in your life where you were no longer as important as your child that was about to be born.

As a mom, eating the right things and taking good care of yourself was all about doing the best for your baby. You took great interest in all of the things you could do to ensure your child had the best chance in life possible. You may have played calming music, engaged in some prenatal yoga, or mind-body training. You sought out a midwife or healthcare team to help with delivery.

You learned quickly that all that seemed to matter was doing your best so your baby was safe and growing and developing. Once born, the task was to ensure psychological and physical safety, nurturing of love and affection, and unconditional acceptance and support. To Parent with Courage you need to understand that the next step is to understand the goal of parenting, which is to prepare your child for the world so that when you are no longer in their lives, they thrive.

You always love your children regardless of how they behave or the path they may choose. The deep love you have does not mean you are afraid to make those often painful decisions that I will be discussing with you at the end of this book.

You take your child for vaccine shots or to the dentist to get a tooth repaired, even though you know they will be in some pain when the procedure is performed. You do this because you know it is in their long-term best interest to feel that brief pain. Just like that, when it comes time to implement your parenting plan, the pain your child may feel is of a short-term nature to ensure long-term growth and development. So Parenting with Courage means you will make those decisions that are in the best interest of your child, even if those decisions mean they will be in pain for a period of time. It takes courage to do this, and I will help you get there.

The second characteristic of Parenting with Courage is that you will understand your child is not your friend, nor will they ever be. You won't confide in them your inner most secrets or your own personal issues or problems because that wouldn't be in the best interest of their future. Parenting with Courage means you understand the need for boundaries and separation as they move through young adulthood. With decision-making there are three levels that I want to explain to you because, as your child grows and develops, Parenting with Courage means you move from one type to the other.

LEVEL 1 DECISION MAKING means you make the decision for them with no input from them whatsoever. You and your spouse or partner discuss the plan of action, but the child has no say in this. If you say you are leaving the restaurant at nine a.m., then you are leaving at nine. You don't ask the child what they think or feel; you insist on leaving at that time. If your child wants to know why, you simply indicate because you are the parent, you made the decision and that is the way it is going to be. Parenting with Courage means you assertively follow through on that promise of leaving at nine.

LEVEL 2 DECISION MAKING means you may ask them their opinion on a decision, but in the end you, and only you, are making that decision, regardless of what their input may be. You outline this before asking them, but in the end, you are going to make the decision. You may ask them what they want to have for dinner tonight, but, ultimately, you would have or prepare what you feel is the best option.

LEVEL 3 DECISIONS are those children make on their own. They may ask you for an opinion, but in the end, they must decide.

11

From birth to later adulthood you would move from a Level 1 to Level 3 decision-making model. Gradually, as you impart confidence in your child for having the strength and intelligence to make independent decisions, they become more comfortable to do so. Parenting with Courage means you understand this needed progression, are strong with younger children being in control, and gradually relinquishing the majority of decision-making as your child moves through later teens and young adulthood.

So let's summarize what Parenting with Courage means:

- Unconditional love for your child, regardless of their behaviour or actions.

- Implementing the strategies needed, even if those strategies may result in brief physical or psychological pain for your child.

- You accept that your child will never be, and should never be, your friend.

- You will make decisions without your child's input, only later to accept the gradual pulling away of control and encouraging their independence.

- You accept that the primary job of parenting your child is to prepare them to thrive once you are no longer available.

3

What is the Makeup of a Strong Leader?

YOU LIKELY HAVE a number of strong leaders around you. It could be your father, mother, a neighbour, or your child's teacher or principal. It could be a business owner in your community. If you think about it, your choices of who to pick out are based on a number of factors. They are what represents strong leadership to you.

I didn't seek out leaders with characteristics as mentioned in publications such as *Harvard Business Review*, sport or organizational psychology. Well, maybe I used a bit of that because I am a psychologist, but mostly I was looking for individuals who demonstrated strong leadership by their actions with family, in their communities, and in their professions or businesses. Here are the important points I considered when choosing whom to interview for this book.

1. Self-confident. There is an internal sense that the person is confident with what they say and do. They often don't have to say anything. You feel this or observe this by their actions. A high self-concept in a specific area such as education, or community leadership or business or sports is demonstrated by action not words. The leaders I interviewed for this project would all be considered very modest by any standard. Many were surprised that I chose to interview them because they were just "doing it," whatever it is they do. Having high self-esteem at something gives you the confidence to lead in that situation or field and empowers others to perform well above their level of usual performance or expertise. Self-esteem is contagious and leaders spew it out to motivate others around them.

2. They live a life that is consistent with their moral and ethical beliefs. This is often called life integrity. If you believe, for example, that all men and women are created equally, what are you doing in your daily life to reflect this? Some would argue that at times we compromise our internal beliefs to accommodate the situation or get that deal or impress someone so that we can benefit. But living with integrity has to do with the actions you take when you decide to enter a situation. If you walk by someone on the street in need of food or clothing, what do you do? Do you walk by? Do you give them your coat in the wintertime? Do

you try to find them a job or invite them to live in a vacant room you have in your house?

If you believe that those on the street need to be helped and we should share what we have, you may choose to do either or all of the suggestions. What you choose to do, even if only giving a loonie, is an action that reflects your beliefs. You understand that there is only so much time in the day to help others, that if you don't take care of your own business you won't be able to help anyone and soon you will be on that street as well. So you choose a path that is consistent with your beliefs and exercise those beliefs in your actions by what you can do.

3. Lead by example. They demonstrate those behaviours they want to see in others. This is a tough concept that weeds out many leaders who don't understand the importance of this concept. With parenting, for example, parents will often tell their teenagers to not use drugs or alcohol while they abuse it themselves. They will tell them to go to school while they take time off work for an illness that doesn't exist. They tell their children to be active yet rarely exercise. Leaders lead by example. They roll up their sleeves and do what is necessary to be successful. They are the first to arrive at work and the last to leave. They don't ask anyone to do anything that they haven't done themselves. The CEO will pick up a paper cup on the lawn if visible while walking into work.

15

4. Take calculated risks. They understand that as leaders they often must decide for the group. The decision they make may not be popular, but it is necessary. They make the best decision based on what they know at the time. No armchair quarterbacking. When the decision doesn't work out, they learn from it; they don't complain or stop taking calculated risks. Leadership within the concept of risk-taking is about understanding that being criticized by others, losing a position or job, and even death may be the consequence of taking a risk for the group. Start a business that eventually fails and watch the people line up, telling you they told you that it wouldn't work out.

In a Fox News documentary on the military action to capture or assassinate Osama Bin Laden, the story is told over and over again of the risks taken that night by the pilots of the helicopters, the military personnel, and other support professionals who had to take risks with little time for long-term planning. The calculated risk of the mission resulted in success with none of the American military injured.

5. Priorities are in place. They place family-spiritual above all else. It may not look that way at times, but if their role is to provide for the family, they will do that while sacrificing all else. Just as living life with integrity, priorities are identified and the predominant amount of time spent working is

on those priorities. If the family is in crisis, the majority of time is placed on working on that.

6. They fight through pain and adversity. It hurts sometimes to make tough decisions. Physical and psychological pain comes and goes, but never guides their decision-making or behaviour. They accept that fighting through pain is part of what they have to do to be strong leaders. Strong leadership is evident when things aren't going well, when there is a crisis or major threat evident. Strong leaders in sports, for example, can never leave a game due to injury. Someone else has to pull them or take them out. In policing, the military, and other first responders, they never want to take themselves out of a situation.

7. Strong work ethic. They out-work most people. This one fascinates me. Is work ethic something that is born or made? All strong leaders have an incredible work ethic. Spending sixty to eighty hours a week on their chosen fields or professions is not unusual.

8. Delay gratification. They are able to delay immediate rewards or wants for long-term gain. They understand the big picture, and while their decision may not always seem popular or the right one at the time, they are within the context of looking at a better outcome for the "team" or "family." Having a vision for what the future should bring and setting goals helps drive this

attitude. Athletes choose to train hours upon hours daily even though the latest video game or friend wanting to go for a coffee pulls on them.

9. Respect for self and others. They respect the opportunities they have and the gifts that they have been given. They have respect for others, especially those less fortunate. They demonstrate compassion and respect, for they can constantly learn from others.

10. Personal sacrifice and toughness. They are willing to sacrifice their own personal rewards or gain for the betterment of the long-term goal or cause. They sacrifice time, energy, and resources because they believe in their long-term desired goal.

11. They never give up or quit. At times even though it's time to move on, it's their decision based on what is best for achieving the goal. If they believe in the cause and that it should continue to be strived for, they never, ever, ever quit.

12. Self-discipline. Discipline learned early in the home transforms to self-discipline and strength later on in life. Making yourself do the things that leaders do comes from within. Athletes with self-discipline know that they need to eat certain foods, exercise a certain way, and practice their skill over and over again. Professional golfers hit over a thousand balls a day using just one club. Strong leaders in sport engage in these disciplined

routines that lead to other teammates or players who see this upping their efforts and performance. Self-discipline is linked to self-criticism where strong leaders self-correct and drive themselves to greater effort.

13. They hate to lose. They are motivated to win. They may define a win differently than most, but once defined, it is the goal. A parent decides that attending every minor hockey game their daughter is involved in is one goal they need to accomplish this year. They adjust schedules and expectations and achieve that goal. The owner of a small business sets the goal of a win being one million dollars in sales. Anything less than that is considered a loss and unacceptable. A college football team sets the goal to win a national championship. Anything less is considered a failed season. Strong leaders set high expectations and believe they will be accomplished.

Strong leaders are made, not born. They are made by what is happening around them, what they watch, what they hear, and how they are parented. You have the power to raise a strong leader. It's not that complicated but will take courage. Do you have the courage to do this?

I travelled to both coasts of Canada and in between to interview the six leaders for this book. Two of them I know and are very close friends and football teammates from college, Claude Riopelle and John Milne. Two of the leaders I met through business or personal contacts, Ho Tek and Gary Waterman, but that was the extent of our relationship. Two of the leaders were total strangers, Kimberley Joines and Natasha Borota, and agreed to meet with me to be interviewed through this project. Suffice it to say, that none of the parents of the leaders in this book knew each other or shared parenting strategies.

Now, let me tell you how to use this book to get the most out of it.

4

How to Use this Book

I HAD A great deal of debate between others and myself with regard to the format of presenting my interviews to you in this book. I was going to summarize them, write them in a different way, but after reading the transcripts, that didn't seem to be the best way to help you understand their stories. So I decided to present the interviews to you with minimal editing and only the quotes that would give you the information you need to understand the leaders' parenting experience.

After you read a chapter I want you to stop and think about it. Write down what you learned about the parenting. After you finish all six of them, compare your answers and see if there are any common themes that jump out at you. For me, many did. I wonder if you will feel the same?

Each interview is, in fact, a collection of "data." At Michigan State University when I was studying group statistics, we were taught that if your sample size (the number of people you are studying) is large enough, you may be able to make conclusions about something that you can then apply to others. Most sample sizes were greater than one hundred, many greater than one thousand, depending on the experiment and what you were looking for. However, it is not uncommon for naturalists or anthropologists to study a small group of people or even individuals. The stories and observations of even one subject can lead to new theories or practices. That's how I want you to use this book. So with each case, think of how specific techniques in parenting impacted that leader's development.

In the last chapters, I tell you my thoughts on what I learned from these interviews that lead to my six strategies for you to Parent with Courage. Write down those strategies and decide how you can implement them in your parenting style. Share the points with your partner, and all of those involved in raising your child, to ensure whatever strategies you choose will be consistent, regardless of who delivers those. If you still aren't sure, sign up for my Parenting with Courage online class found at www.drsvec.com. You can take it any time to learn specific ways you can help your child become a strong leader.

5

Claude Riopelle

SPORTS CAN TEACH us many things. It is a theme you will read about in many of the leaders I interviewed for this book. Being involved in team sports can lead to strong leadership skills because it teaches discipline, team as opposed to individual accomplishments, and strong work ethic. Respect for authority is also implemented in many sports organizations. Claude "Ripper" Riopelle is an example of how sports involvement leads to developing outstanding leadership skills.

I first met Claude in the summer of 1975. I was a freshman at the University of Western Ontario trying out for their football team. Ripper was an established player, and gradually over the three years that we played beside each other on the defensive line, he taught me many lessons. When we parted ways, we kept in touch on and off throughout the years. Claude is a strong leader on many fronts. He led in his days as a player on the football field at Western. He finished one season playing with a broken jaw, leading us to a national championship. As a player, he was a quiet leader, often leading by example, and off the field ensuring that many of the social activities fit with building camaraderie and a winning team. In education, he led his teams to many conference championships, and as a teacher, helped thousands of children achieve their potential despite their special needs.

In his community, Claude continues to lead by example. A near-death experience led to a drastic change in lifestyle and is an example to us all, of our obligation to family.

At the University of Western Ontario, Claude was a member of national championship teams in 1974, 1975, and 1976. In 1976 and 1977 he was named to the All-Canadian team, meaning he was one of the best defensive lineman in the country. He was drafted by the Winnipeg Blue Bombers. In 2012, he was named to the North Bay Sports Hall of Fame and the University of Western Ontario "W" Club Hall of Fame. He was named to the Wall of Champions at TD Waterhouse Stadium for his football excellence.

After graduation he worked as a high school teacher and football coach in St. Thomas, Toronto, and Barrie. He successfully coached Innisdale Secondary School to seven GBSSA titles and Stayner to two. I interviewed Ripper at a coffee shop in Collingwood, Ontario.

He was born September 3, 1953 in Mattawa, Ontario,

which is just outside North Bay. Soon after his birth his family moved to North Bay. His father was a journeyman carpenter and his mother a homemaker.

Claude discusses the work ethic he viewed in his father.

He always worked hard. Never hung out. Like being a carpenter means you're waiting for one union job then another. My dad worked on almost every house on our street in North Bay, because he's a carpenter. So neighbours trusted him to do the steps, fence, and I'm trying to do the same thing up here, so I'm kind of proud of that. He was never without work and always did whatever, like shoveling snow off roofs in the wintertime, like anything for a buck.

Ripper worked with his father at an early age.

I always worked with him, yeah. Well, when I was available I'd do carpentry with him, and in the wintertime on a Saturday, Sunday, when I was there, I'd be shoveling roofs with him.

I asked about his grandparents, wondering where his father learned his work ethic.

My grandpa on my mom's side was a musician and an intellectual. I don't know what else he did. I think he taught music and stuff. But on my dad's side, he was a farmer up in Mattawa, which is not very prosperous for farming; it's rugged up there.

With regard to discipline growing up, Ripper reports that his brothers experienced more structure and discipline than he did, but suggested he was well aware of who was in charge and the rules.

I guess I had a favourable background because my dad was really, really tough on the group of five, my older siblings and I knew enough what to do and what not to do. Because he was a journeyman, he worked out of town a lot, so Mom was mostly responsible for things. I knew what the guidelines were and the parameters were and stuff, it was pretty well laid out. I was no angel, but I knew where to go, how far to go.

I asked Claude about his experience as a child, getting everything he wanted or needed.

Put it this way, I never did without, but I knew if I lost something, that was it. So I didn't lose anything because it wouldn't be replaced, like, to this day I don't lose a hockey stick, I don't lose anything, any of my stuff. No, I was taken care of that way, but as I said, I appreciated stuff, and I guess my parents grew up during the Depression, so they really knew what a dollar meant.

I asked Ripper again where he thought he learned his work ethic and if it was from his parents.

Yeah and my mom. My mom was hardworking too, like, you know, doing clothes by hand. I remember stuff like that, hanging stuff out on the line because we didn't have a dryer. Never had a dishwasher. I think your work ethic is established through your parents, I'm sure. My daughter just gave me the greatest compliment. She said, "If you didn't teach me anything else, you taught me hard work."

Given that sports were very important for Claude during his formative years throughout university, I asked him how he got started, and what lead to his path of playing football.

Football, hockey, and basketball in high school. After about one year of basketball, the coach said, "Stick to hockey."

On playing hockey:

There was no fighting in high school hockey. But I was the enforcer. I looked after things, but no, no fighting. I was never a fighter. It wasn't in my DNA; however, all of my brothers are wired that way.

Claude discusses his early experiences with football and how close he came to choosing a different path.

Well, the biggest setback I had, which most people would think was an advantage, is I went to the same high school as my brothers. So the expectation was you're going to play and my next two oldest brothers were pretty good football players, and Rene actually played for Hamilton (of the CFL). So the reputation preceded them, so when I went in, I said I'm not sure if I want to play. And, of course, you're playing, and I got out there, and I was a little timid. That's when grade elevens could still play junior football, like, wow, we had guys with beards playing against us. The effective change, and I thought about this because I knew you'd ask me, my brother Irvin came home after being cut by the Argos and he says, "Well, how's the football going?" I said, "You want to know the truth? Sometimes I'm scared to death." And he said to me, "Hmmm." And I didn't know what he'd say, and he goes, "You know what, if you're afraid, you probably should quit playing."

That wasn't what I expected he'd say. He said, "You know what, if you're not afraid of something, you'll be just fine. If you hit somebody harder than they hit you, you'll always come out ahead." I bought it one hundred percent. So the next practice on the Monday, I went out from being like 'where are we going to put this guy' and I worked my way through to being a starter. I guess first week was kick-off, kick-off return, that sort of thing, and then I end up playing for the rest of the year, but that was the turning point. It was something that clicked because I really loved the game.

On playing college football at the University of Western Ontario:

I was going to Ottawa, I didn't even apply to Western. Lead Boots (Curtis Rush) was the best player out in North Bay the year before I played, and I looked and I played a little senior football with him, so I knew him pretty well. So in the summertime, we were working out together and he says, "Well, what are you doing next year?" I said, "I'm going to Ottawa." He asked if I had visited Western yet, and I said no.

So how do I get to Western? It just happened that Cosentino was the head coach, a good, personal friend of my brother Rene. They played together in Hamilton, got me in to King's College because it was the Catholic college.

I asked him the progression from freshman to All-Canadian defensive lineman.

That was a little disheartening because I went out as a linebacker, which I think was the best position for me. But after I made the team, Rick Scarborough (later to become the best fullback in Canada and in the Western W Club Hall of Fame as well) got cut, which was crazy. So anyways, I don't know why I made the team, but I thought I had a pretty good camp. I was ninth at the start of the camp, and at the end of the season, I was still ninth. And then they had the Colts team that year, so I went to the Colt's practice on a Friday and they played a Saturday game against Seneca or Sheridan who had football back then, and Reggie might have been one of the head coaches, and of course, now I'm down at the Colts, I'm not starting.

So one of the D lineman goes down and, remember, I never played D line, I didn't even know a three-point stance or four-point stance. Reggie looks around and says he needs a D lineman, and they didn't have any depth. So I jumped up and said I'm in. And I end up just with my regular skills and aggression and stuff. I got a couple of tackles, sack and all, filmed. The next game I'm the starting defence tackle, they play another team, and coincidently, I sacked a guy that I end up playing ball with up in Barrie, like, slow pitch. I was probably about 235. We were never that big, but that's the sizes right, it worked. And then the next year they had me penciled in to start, so that's how it goes.

Claude explains his decision to play with a broken jaw. I have a number of personal memories from that year. The main one that continues to come up when I think of his sacrifice is my looking over at Claude at practice with his wired jaw, thinking of how tired I am. How I don't want to practice. But when I see him giving one hundred percent, even though he's eating out of a straw and the coaches have to have wire cutters in case he starts choking in practice, I feel guilty and suck it up. I still believe to this day that the leadership that Claude displayed lead us to our next National Championship that year.

It was a no brainer on my part. If there was any reason I could play, I'd play. You played the same position; I didn't want to give up my spot. I wanted to play. My mom and dad never interfered with sports. I think we had faith or confidence in a medical professional. If the wires had gotten dislodged, the bone would have gone up through my brain. Maybe I was a little crazy.

I continued to ask Claude if he saw himself as a leader.

I try to be. I might have been considered for captain,

which I consider a leader, but I never was because I was a little bit crazy. I understood a long time ago the importance of team and that no one person is bigger than that.

After football, I asked Claude about his next life challenges.

Well, probably after Mary and I committed and were together, was getting a job. I just thought everything came along, like a progression and you're sitting there at Teacher's College at U of T, and you're the same era as me, there weren't a lot of teaching jobs, similar to now. Ten people were up for the job. And I figured, well, I guess that's me. Sorry about the other nine, but that's the way I thought.

This internal confidence, the belief that he would be the one out of ten that got that teaching job reflects a type of optimism that is a strong leadership trait. It is the type of belief system that is contagious. If you are around that long enough, you start to believe as Claude does, that anything is possible. I don't have an answer to the question, "Was Claude born with this trait or was it developed over time with his exposure to his parents' example and later football experiences?" I'm thinking it's a combination of things, some genetics, some random chance, and likely fifty percent or more of what he witnessed growing up.

Near the end of Claude's teaching career, I was fortunate to meet him at his high school for a brief visit. While walking down the hall of his school many students stopped to say hi or ask what was up or how he was doing. I asked him how he developed this type of rapport with the student body.

It doesn't come easy, but I'll tell you, coaching is one of the greatest things that teachers could ever do, because kids respect coaches, whether you're coaching them or not. They see you out there, they know you're interested, they know it's on your time, and they appreciate that. It's kind of like that, and over the course of all the years I've taught, because teaching technology and shops I didn't teach very many females, they all knew I was a coach. You walk into your shop class day one, and you see five kids that you saw at practice at football. They're in your class, the tone of the class is set, because no one's going to screw up.

I asked Claude if he had noticed a change in the character of the students he was teaching from the time he started teaching to his recent retirement.

Yeah, really. As a matter of fact, one of the finest things is I worked at Stayner for nine years at the high school, so Stayner kids all live in this area. I go to buy stone the other day for my driveway, and the kid working at the desk was one of my students, so you have a rapport, you're happy they're doing well. You chat him up, and at the end of the day, the guy gives you a discount, and you go out the door like you're an MVP. It's good.

Next, I ask Claude about his near-death experience and his current challenges.

Right now, the challenge I'm dealing with is the body's breaking down, which I always look at in a positive spin. I did a lifestyle change three years ago. I knew I could do it, and I was thinking about it and, sometimes, you need an event. So I had my event (he stopped breathing), and I'm not that dumb that I figured out the first was how much Mary means to me and seeing my kids grow up. And, hopefully, see your kids have kids and stuff. Or you just discount all that and carry on your stupid lifestyle. I was too heavy, probably did a lot of things in excess. I smoked for a long time, which was really dumb. But quitting drinking was easy compared to quitting smoking. I still think about smoking, that's one of the toughest demons that you can ever get rid of.

That's the part that's hardest on me. The first challenge I had, and I quit drinking late January. The challenging part is guys who don't understand, and they go, "When are you going to have a drink?" I tell them I'm not doing that anymore. I've hit my quota, matter of fact, I probably hit my quota ten years ago. I'm moving on.

The quiet leadership for Claude continues as he models a healthier lifestyle for his family, friends, and community. He doesn't push what he's doing or tell others to change their habits, but gently nudges them to understand what he is doing and perhaps with that, lead them to a better life. I ask him if he believes leaders just do their thing and live their life, or do they get up each day intentionally striving to lead others.

No, I didn't do it for a purpose, but in retrospect, I understand that those things worked out favourably. I didn't coach for thirty years because that was a grandstand year.

I realized that I liked doing it. Now the part that comes with it is the respect, and that works out really well for you. With the being a leader on a football team, when I was playing, I looked at it as if it made us all better, that's the way to go.

I don't know white-collar; I don't really know it. I just know that my dad worked hard for everything he did, and he didn't give up. The scary part was when he was fixing something of mine, whether it was a bike or a Transformer, he was pretty good at fixing stuff.

I asked Claude how he handles situations where he may need to stop or give up on something. Fact of the matter is he hates to lose.

Oh shit, everybody has shit go through their head, but it doesn't stick. Seriously, I did let it stick. I'm a positive, upbeat guy; everybody has challenges. I have a really supportive, great wife. That's a real good one, and I look at her and I go, I do appreciate her a lot and I thank you. I always thought I was a team guy, even when I played men's slow pitch. I always wanted to put the team before myself. You hit a lousy ball, I don't sit there and walk to first base. I would hustle down and try to beat the throw. I mean you try to make up for that. It's contagious.

I ask Claude about having children and how his own childhood is impacting the parenting of his children.

Well, Mom looked after everything. I was no angel. I got disciplined at school a lot. I would never tell them at home I got disciplined at school, because that's the old days, right, you'll get nailed again. So I took my lumps. When I go back to North Bay, there are two of my teachers I want to track down. I haven't seen them in a while. I want to thank them.

And with my kids, we gave them support. My daughter's going to Alaska. Well, Mary and I looked at each other, and she's on Skype, so we're looking at her, we've got to celebrate she got a job and stuff, but Mary's really looking at Alaska. How about Toronto? But we don't say that because that's not helping the cause. How you help the cause, we're going to go visit you. You got it all together. So, giving independence.

On disciplining his own children today:

Firm and fair is what I try. We never touched our kids, that was a decision we made, and I'm not opposed to that. Sometimes, you know you need a little straightening out. But our kids are both sensitive enough, extremely sensitive. You just raised your voice and…

I asked him about parents today and strategies that don't seem to be working.

I think a lot of people want to give their kids everything and that's not a good way to go.

When asked why he thinks that is the case:

I have no idea, maybe they've always wanted stuff or

maybe they were given stuff. If you're given things too easily that's not good. It's good to earn.

I asked Claude about his future goals.

I'm hoping I'm healthy enough as the guy that walked in here, Butch. He's still working as a dentist [Butch came over to talk while we were doing the interview at the coffee shop], he's mid seventies, he rides as much as he can, he is proud of his accomplishments, he's doing great. Does he look fit? Extremely fit. That's what I want to be. I want to be healthy, but you know what I realized when I made my lifestyle change? There are certain things you can control: your fitness level, your nutrition, your lifestyle, your emotions. You can't control a hip, a shoulder, maybe I wore them out, but don't let it stop you. Keep moving forward.

Final thoughts on his own parenting style now:

Well, as I said Marissa (daughter) kind of gave me the supreme compliment, she says, "You and mom work so hard, that's where I get it from." And Ryley (daughter) she's a great employee, she works really hard; she doesn't let them down. I think so many people just take the easy way out and they phone in sick, this and that, having a bad day, drank too much red wine last night.

* * *

So to summarize:

- Ripper grew up in an environment where he witnessed a strong work ethic in both of his parents, linked to his grandparents.

- He understood the rules and expectations of the home.

- He understood his place and the role of his father and mother in the home.

- He led by example in all aspects of his athletic and professional life.

- He tolerated pain and controversy better than others.

- He sacrificed for the team and learned early on that when you work hard and help others, you elevate the entire team.

- He is competitive and doesn't like to lose.

- He didn't get everything he wanted as a child nor did he give that to his children, even though economically he was able.

- He attributes his children's work ethic today as a significant part of their success.

- He continues to lead in his community by his example and professional skills by helping others.

6

Gary Waterman

GARY WATERMAN IS the forty-seven-year-old head football coach at St. Francis Xavier University in Antigonish, Nova Scotia. He is the first black head football coach in the Atlantic Conference's history and only the fourth ever to be named that position in Canada. This year his team won the Atlantic Conference championship for the first time since 1996 and represented the east in the Canadian championship semifinal against the eventual champion, the UBC Thunderbirds. Gary is an outstanding coach and leader of young men. What he did in the community when horrific tragedy struck Antigonish is an example of his strong leadership and testament to his character and integrity. He is a strong leader on many fronts.

Ottilia Chareka was a professor in the Faculty of Education at St. Francis Xavier University. On March 16, 2011, at the age of forty-two, Ottilia was murdered by her husband in her home. Prior to this fatal date, a video was made that features Ottilia. It can be found here https://youtu.be/SXHaWpbvVrY. I strongly recommend you watch this seven-minute production before you read on.

Daughters lost their mother that night and then their father when he was sentenced to a life in prison. Children left without parents. What would Gary Waterman have to do with this?

I interviewed Gary Waterman in his office at St. Francis Xavier University in Antigonish.

"I started (coaching) right away. Well, actually I started coaching back in high school. I was always involved. I always loved coaching. When I was in grade twelve, my high school did not have a track team, so I tried to get that going."

You started coaching at what age?

I've always been involved with community activities and coaching younger kids, I always enjoyed just being part sports. When I was in high school, I was at a school where they didn't have a track program. I decided that I wanted to get it going. I started organizing and running practices. I loved doing it. When I graduated from high school I went to St. FX. During the summer months, I would go back to Mississauga and work for Mississauga

Park and Recreation. I ran a teen summer drop-in community centre, and I began coaching there.

Because you played here for four years?

Yes.

How was that experience?

Overall, it was great, but at the beginning I wasn't sure if St. FX was the right choice because I didn't know anything about Nova Scotia at the time. When I was in grade eleven, I was selected to represent my high school at the Ontario Student Leadership Camp in Lake Couchiching. At the time, almost every high school in Ontario was able to send one representative to the Leadership program. While I was at the camp, I met a guy named Joe Jurus. Joe was another Mississauga guy who attended De La Salle, an all boys' high school in Toronto. At the camp, Joe and I became very good friends. He ended up coming out to Nova Scotia and St. FX a year before I did. He loved his first year experience at St. FX.

We actually bumped into each other again during the summer after his freshman year, and he asked me where I was going to go to school the upcoming year. I told him that I had not decided yet, and immediately, he responded with St. FX. So we started talking, and eventually, I talked to the head football coach, and the next thing you know, one thing lead to another, and I ended up coming out to St. FX. When I first got out here, it

DR. HENRY J. SVEC

seemed like a really small community, it was not as developed as it is now. I remember saying to myself "where the heck am I?" being from a community much bigger than the town of Antigonish.

Had you ever been out east before?

No, it was my first time.

Because you're from Toronto?

Yeah. I was born in Toronto, but I grew up in Mississauga. When I made the final decision to come out to St. FX for school, I just grabbed my suitcases, got on a plane, and jumped on a bus to Antigonish. Really, everything happened pretty fast, but I said to myself, let's just go for it. When I arrived on campus, the football team was already on the field. So I walked over to the team with my two bags and my jacket over my arm and met a bunch of people for the first time. The rest is history. I ended up slowly starting to really like St. FX and the town of Antigonish. I played my entire university career at St. FX.

You were DB, right?

I played defensive back and running back. I had played both in high school, and when I came into camp I told them that I would play wherever they needed me to play. They basically decided to give me a shot at running back because they had lost one of their running backs from the previous year. I said no problem and started playing running back. I had a great exhibition game, and after that took over the job as the starting running back. I did that job for a number of years before I started playing some defensive back as well. I ended up playing both ways for a little bit. Eventually, I transitioned to playing defensive back and only being spotted on offensive.

What was the last game you ever played?

I think it was St. Mary's. Yeah, it was my fourth year, and it was a home game versus St. Mary's. I had hurt my ankle the week before, at Acadia. It was the first time I've had any type of serious injury. It was a high ankle sprain. I was just trying to gut it out during my last game because I wanted to play badly. I played through the pain and only returned kicks and played a little bit on defence. I was on a wonky ankle.

So you graduate school then, what do you do?

After I graduated from St. FX University, I decided to go back to Mississauga. I started coaching football right away. It was the Father Michael Goetz High School summer camp. I had a couple of friends and ex-teammates that had already graduated from St. FX and were coaching there.

Were you married yet?

No. My wife and I met at St. FX University. She was in nursing and I was in human kinetics. We were actually in the same first year biology class together, but we never really knew each other. It wasn't until two or three years later when we kind of first met and started dating. Once we both graduated, we decided to move out to Mississauga, and I started coaching right away.

Were you a teacher?

I graduated with a teaching degree from St. FX, and I was trying to get a job back in Mississauga. It was after my fourth year of university. I had come back home to Mississauga, and that same year John Stevens became the new head football coach at St. FX. He was the former defensive coordinator and got promoted to head coach. When I first got home to Mississauga, I find out at the time that my father (grandfather) was ill with cancer. He was not given very long to live. Around the same time, unknowingly, John was trying to convince me to return to St. FX for my final year of eligibility.

It's the goal of most college coaches to try to get the better football players back for an additional year. However, because I had learned the news about the health of my father, I did not feel I could return. I needed to be home for support. I never ended up going back. In one final attempt to convince me to return, John mentioned the possibility of me going the coaching route. He would mentor me and help develop me as an assistant coach. He actually asked me if I would be interested in coming back in that capacity. In retrospect, I am sure he felt that if I agreed to come back as a coach, that the itch to play would be so strong that eventually I would end up just playing out my final year anyway. I did not end up coming back to St. FX in the coaching capacity, and that same year they hired an unknown coach at the time named Blake Nill. Well, if anyone knows anything about Blake Nill, I think St. FX and Coach Nill did just fine without me.

Anyway, I ended up not coming back for my final year and stayed home in Mississauga. Eventually, my father did lose his battle with cancer, and I officially began my teaching and coaching career at home.

And meanwhile you're still coaching high school?

I was still teaching and coaching at Father Michael Goetz High School in Mississauga. I coached football, basketball, and track.

And teaching, too?

I was teaching and coaching. I loved coaching and coached almost every different sport at one time or another. It was fun. Several years later, a new coach was hired at St. FX. His name was John Bloomfield. On an Ontario recruiting trip, John came out to Mississauga to meet with me. I had been at a high school blessed with some very talented university football prospects. On his visit to my high school, John invited me to become a guest coach during his spring football camp. I had not been back on the St. FX campus for a long time, so I jumped at the opportunity. I went out and coached that first camp and really enjoyed my experience.

They liked the work I did and invited me back for several other camps. John wanted to get me out here permanently, and the players seemed to like my coaching style as well. I told them that if I could find a job teaching out there, then I would be interested in moving out to Nova Scotia. We started looking at the possibilities, and the athletic director, Leo MacPherson, played a big role in making it happen. I got a teaching job. I decided to take a year's leave of absence from teaching high school in Mississauga and began teaching junior high school in Antigonish. I ended up teaching during the day and working as the St. FX defensive coordinator in the evening. I started that in 2006.

You're married at the time?

Yes. Andrea and I were married, and her family is from Truro, Nova Scotia. She was very excited to come home. Everything just made sense because we had so many ties to Nova Scotia. We always came back every Christmas and during the summers as well. We seemed to always be back in Truro.

So, then you're named head coach. When was that?

I interviewed and was offered the St. FX head football coaching job in 2009.

And despite all the black football players in Canada, and the world, you were the second, or first ever, head coach?

I was the first black head football coach in AUS and St. FX history and the fourth ever in the CIS.

Did you find that strange? You know, I never asked you about this. How do you feel about that?

I think there was a sense of pride in the African-Canadian community, but for me, I kind of kept plugging along and never stopped to look at it that way.

You just do your thing?

Yes, I just kind of tried to do my thing. I was so focused on trying to do a good job that I never really looked at it or thought about it. I think that when my coaching career eventually comes to an end, I will have time to reflect back on everything and evaluate all of it.

It is important.

Yeah. I never thought about it much. I have never been that type of person to sort of stop during my work and think about the significance of it. Although, I think in my first year I had no choice to think about it for at least one game because we ended up playing Bishops University. At the time, Leroy Blue was their head football coach. Leroy is another African-Canadian CIS head football coach. We were going head-to-head. It was only the

DR. HENRY J. SVEC

second time in CIS football history where two black head football coaches had an opportunity to coach against each other. For many, it was a very significant moment. The game was covered by Cabbie who was working with the Score television network at the time. He did a feature on the game. It was a great experience for all.

You don't even think about it?

No, it became more of a bigger deal for the press.

What about for your players who are black, do you think there is something?

I think for some of them, on a deeper level I think, there is a sense of pride. I think they see that coaching at a high level can become a reality for them. They can actually see a pathway to do it.

You don't even think about it?

I don't have time in this world to slow down.

So this year, you folks win. You're one of the top four teams in the country.

Yeah.

And there are only two games on TV, and one of them is yours. First time, I think, ever?

Yes.

How did you feel about that one?

Well, we were really excited. I mean, it's the first time in nineteen years that we had won the Loney Bowl. If you know our history, we've had some good players here throughout the years. For whatever the reason, we just couldn't get it done. After the game I said on an interview, "This win is not just for the players that are here, but all the people that were here before them that deserved a better fate." Over that nineteen-year time frame, we lost a lot of close games that could have led to some other championships.

Tell me about the leaders. Do you consider yourself a strong leader or you kind of just do it? You just grind and whatever happens, happens?

No, you know, I think leadership for me has been something whereas I have always had natural personal leadership qualities, but I think I've learned over the years that leading a large team is a big challenge. I've had to work at it and learn to become a better leader of people. You know, I've always lead by doing things, but it takes a while. I think you have to work at learning to lead people, which I think is completely different.

So you not only win this year, which is amazing. Nineteen years, you had some great players, you get players playing everywhere, NFL, it's all over the wall here. One of the things you did in the community, which was incredible, was when tragedy hit, you took care of some folks. Can you talk a little bit about that?

Out of respect for the privacy of the family, I don't want to get into details of the events or the names of the children. However, I am completely amazed at how special and resilient I think the family is. For us, getting involved and having a couple of the children live with us just seemed like the right thing. Again, it's not one of those things you think about or are ever prepared for.

What makes it right to you?

Well, you know you look at people in need, and you say to yourself, "I have the ability to make a difference or help, and it's not going to hurt me, so why not." This whole situation made sense for our family.

So, if we step back to what childhood was like with you. What was it like growing up?

For me it's kind of a weird thing, I grew up with my grandparents, not my parents. I know who my mother is, but I've never met my dad.

Was it her parents you were with or your dad's?

It was her parents that raised me. At one point, my biological mother had married a man who was enlisted in the US military. They moved around quite a bit. I have a brother who is a couple years younger than me. He was born in California and grew up with our mother. They were stationed in California, Germany, and a few other military bases. As a child, I had been out to visit them on the US base in Germany.

So how did she not have you?

She had me when she was younger, and they all thought that the best thing for me was for my grandparents to raise me.

Was there any discipline growing up?

Yeah, there was discipline but not heavy-handed discipline.

Did you ever get spanked?

I remember distinctly getting hit once or twice, but for my grandparents, it wasn't something where it was an iron fist type of discipline. I never got the iron fist, but I remember getting touched up a few times if I did something silly.

What did your grandparents do for a living?

They both worked for the postal service. They worked as postal workers for thirty-five years, and my grandfather was a postal worker and worked at night at a steel company. He had two jobs. I remember them getting up and going to work every day. They were hard workers. One of my moments that I remember is when they got their thirty-five year service pins. They got up every day, and they went to work. It was good lesson.

You did the same thing?

Yeah, you never know it at the time, but when you see people getting up, going to work, and never complaining about it, it impacts you. There is something admirable about people who take pride in their job and do it well. It is impressive.

Did you get everything you wanted growing up?

Yes. Almost everything.

Did you hear the word no?

At times, but they were good to me. I don't remember going without anything.

Where did they put you in your sports?

I always remember running around outside and just being faster than everybody else and playing games like Red Rover and British Bulldog. The other kids could not catch me. Soccer was the first organized sport that I played. I must have been eight or nine. I thought I was a pretty good soccer player. I played hockey after that. Good Canadian kid, playing hockey. I was not a bad hockey player either. I was captain of the hockey team a couple of seasons. Eventually, I started playing other sports like basketball, track, and football. Football was the thing that finally won my heart and hooked me.

Who was in charge at home?

I'd say, ultimately, the person that did most of the heavy lifting around the house was my mother (grandmother). She was the glue and did everything.

You see her as your mother?

Yes, I say my mother. Sometimes I say grandmother just for reference, but I always called them my mother and father because they raised me.

How tough was it when your mom passed away?

That was tough. It was tough for me because after some-one passes that means a lot to you, you begin to reflect about all of the good times and things that they have done for you. You feel like you are going to be alone. My parents (grandparents) raised me. They stepped up and did a great job, and I have nothing but love and admiration for who they were and their flaws as well. It was really sad to see that they were both gone, because it feels like part of who they were is gone as well.

Do you think you were spoiled?

I think so. I think I was spoiled. I have to look back and say yes, I think I was spoiled because I didn't want for anything. I don't remember wanting for anything. I was the only child in the household, so there's no one else to compete with.

How do you find it your grandparents took care of you, and then when there's a tragedy here, you stepped up and took care of someone else?

I never made any connection until you just mentioned that. I never thought about it. Well, I think there's probably some element deep down, maybe subconsciously, you just do the right thing. You don't think about things when you are in the moment, you have an opportunity to make a decision of whether you can help someone else out, and you react. You do the right thing. Your life situation at the time allows you to help. Maybe sometimes you're in a different situation, and there's no possible way to do it. We were there, we were connected, and their family was in need.

What advice would you give parents who have kids and want to raise strong leaders? What would you tell them they need to do?

I think you've got to be there for your kids. Nurture them. I think they're going to make some mistakes. I don't think you want to do everything for them, I think they need to find their way, and you need to understand that you can't live their lives for them or fix every mistake that they make. Our job as parents is to teach them how to fly alone.

Ten years from now, where's Gary Waterman?

Ten years from now, I hope to be coaching kids. I mean,

wherever it is, whatever level it is. I like doing it. I love working with people trying to affect their lives and helping them. I hope to be coaching somewhere, that's what I would be like doing.

* * *

Gary Waterman watched his grandparents work and struggle—not knowing they weren't his biological parents until he was ten or eleven years of age. He was raised in a house with discipline but only experienced corporal punishment on a few isolated times. He reported in the interview that he felt that he didn't need anything, or want anything, growing up but didn't receive everything he asked for. We have no information on the state of his biological mother's life while she was carrying Gary, but we may guess that there was some anxiety or life uncertainty present during that time in her life.

He watched his parents (grandparents) give to others and help within the community. What he witnessed growing up was very much like the natural step he and his wife took in caring for other children when tragedy struck in 2011. While I knew Gary through visiting on a few prior occasions, this interview with him was life changing for me. This amazing man living in Antigonish "just doing it" but changing lives every day, leading by example, not words.

7

Ho Tek

HO TEK IS a thirty-two-year-old entrepreneur from Waterloo, Ontario. He is a principal partner in Domus Housing, a service business in Waterloo that manages rental properties across the country. He joined the firm as a partner in 2007 and worked to help it grow to becoming a multimillion-dollar business. In 2012, Ho and his partner were nominated for Ernst and Young's Young (under thirty) Entrepreneur of the Year, in recognition of their outstanding performance in their industry.

Ho is a leader in business, in his community, and within his family. Currently, his firm Domus Housing has over three thousand beds under management. They are the largest independent student-housing provider in Waterloo, Ontario. They have signed contracts to manage properties in Windsor, Kingston, London, Kitchener, and St. Catharines. They are also starting to expand to Western

Canada, recently signing with a firm in Kelowna, British Columbia. Ho and his team deal with typical renter complaints, often magnified by the fact that the majority of his tenants are students attending college or university.

I interviewed Ho at his offices in Waterloo. I began the interview by asking Ho about his current workweek obligations and business.

"A typical workweek is a good forty hours, for sure, up and down as much as I need to, and lately, because the second kid just came three weeks ago, I have been trying to cut back on those hours just to be with my wife a little bit more, but that is it. It is a forty-hour workweek generally. We do have a lot of team members who are here to help us with everything that comes up. When we first started off, it was a sixty-hour workweek with Tara and I. It was just Tara and I, and everything was done through us—the late night phone calls, all of the issues that came up, flooding houses. It was just two people, but now we are at a point where we have enough people to take care of the issues that do come up, because they always come up."

In the 1980s, the Canadian Government accepted tens of thousands of refugees from Cambodia who were trying to escape communism. Ho's mother was pregnant with him when they escaped and came to Canada. She experienced anxiety and significant emotional upheaval as anyone would engaged in such a lifesaving attempt to flee a country.

Ho discusses the lessons he later learned from that experience:

Yes, it is really interesting. We are immigrants, right. So they always have this line that they told us, and they still have this suitcase—it is humungous—and it is a gray suitcase, and they are like "This is what we came over with from Cambodia, and the only thing that we had in there was all of our worldly possessions were in half of it, and in the other half was a bag of rice because you had to have food in order to come here." We got sponsored by the Canadian Government, so there was a few places that you could go, and we won the lottery because they would randomly draw names, and we came to Canada. They were dropped off in Edmonton, which was super cold.

Very early in life, Ho watched his father work hard to get ahead.

He started off as a candy maker, and I think he got paid something crazy like $2.75 an hour, and then he realized quickly that that does not make sense, so he started working at a leather factory. He would wrap his hands with masking tape because it was affordable. They worked hard, and then eventually they got a job working at a high school. My dad would work as a jeweler, he was a goldsmith, and he was trained in Canada for that because my uncle was a jeweler with a company, and then he would work all day, and then drive an hour out to the high school and then he would work the night shift with my mother. We were left at a very young age to sort of like fend for ourselves at home. We were not allowed to open the door, pick up the phone, or anything. We knew that my dad would call at four thirty every single day, and Terri and I would do that, and then my brothers…

I saw that my parents were really hard workers. When they were working at the high school, I was like, "Why would you do that, why would you work so hard like that?" They were also one of the first in their group to buy a house. That was something else that was really revolutionary, once you learn about it when you grow up. Everybody else was still in government housing. We were in government housing for over a couple of years, and then my dad was like, "No, the only way it makes sense is if you buy a house."

His friends were all like, "You are an idiot, why would you do that? There is no point. You can just keep on living off the government." But, my dad's thing was that there is no reason, like in Canada, there is no reason why you should be on unemployment, there is no reason why you should need the government's support if you are able-bodied and can work.

During the interview, I began to feel that while Ho deeply respected his father, his father influenced him from an early age on what it meant to live life with character. Discipline may appear to be harsh by today's standards, but what Ho experienced was not unusual for a strong parent to adminis-

ter given the knowledge at the time. When asked about discipline, Ho replied:

Oh yeah, we joke around about this all the time. I was spanked if I did something wrong. As the firstborn son in an immigrant family, you have to be ready to step up and step in when it comes time. So I was very disciplined, and it was strict. He ruled with an iron fist. My mom worked, my dad worked, and whatever my dad said sort of went. It was really weird. I hung out with my girlfriend at the time, and they were talking about what they would do during the Christmas break, so they sat down and said, "Oh, we could go to the ROM, we could go to AGO, and all this stuff," and I was so perplexed. The way that it works in my family is, you get in the minivan and you go wherever your parents are telling you to go. But over here, it was like, no let's sit down and talk about it, so it was so strange. It wasn't until probably about four or five years ago that he started to not give me advice. He still gives me a lot of advice, he still parents, but now it is like the other way around, where we are always talking and we are always throwing ideas back and forth to see how to best proceed.

Along with the strong sense of discipline within the home, Ho was denied many of the things other children and teens learned to expect. At the time, he reports to have resented it deeply, including his father not giving him the opportunity to play sports, but now he feels that it was a good lesson learned.

They (children) are denied a lot of things because, no, of course, it's healthy, because what are you going to do if you are denied something. If you really want it, then you are going to find a way to go out and get it yourself, because then you have found a way to do it yourself, right. That is really it. That is so important. If you really think it is that important to go out and get a nose ring for example, if you found a way to do it, go ahead, but I am not supporting it (getting a nose ring) and the answer is no. One of the things that they taught us was the value of money.

You saved up and you would buy lunch and you would buy video games and things like that, but it took forever. You would work a month to get a video game, and then you would realize quickly, this absolutely sucks. My dad at a very young age said, "You got to go out there and get a job." His biggest thing is, "You just got to do something different. Don't go out there and work at a donut shop, don't go out there and work at a grocery store or whatever everyone is doing. Do something different and that will put you ahead."

There was an ad in the newspaper for baking donuts and that was when they still baked donuts, but it is a really tough job. You don't actually bake anything; you deep-fry it all. I would work from Friday night from seven or eight at night until six in the morning. It was really good because you got to go in there, create your own systems, really be efficient at it and everything, and I kept on doing that, but the greatest thing was everyone else was making six twenty-five an hour, and I got paid ten dollars an hour, which was a lot of money at that time. I still remember the biggest thing about our family was you sort of pool all your money together. My dad never asked for it, but you always gave it to him, but he also gave us at a very young age a credit card, so we could spend whatever we wanted on there; we knew we had to pay for it eventually.

Having been brought up in a strict disciplined environment the question of self-esteem arises. Many child-rearing experts point to the need for more permissive parenting strategies to ensure strong self-concept development in children. Ho's experience runs immediately opposite to that, but he presents and displays a strong, quiet sense of self-confidence. I wondered how that transpired. His confidence appears to come from the fact that he believes, and has demonstrated, he has control over his future. He knows that success for him is directly linked to a strong work ethic, something he learned from his mother and father. He discusses the belief that part of his drive comes from his opinion that he is limited when it comes to conventional academic environments.

I am very self-confident, for sure. If you were to ask a lot of people, I am pretty cocky. The thing I realize now, is that you have to work hard for everything you want. It doesn't just come.

When the subject of what is rewarded by his parents, or valued, Ho talks a great deal about what is expected. It's as if he knew his role, knew what was expected of him and the con-

sequences of what would happen if he failed. The power of parents to establish this environment and shape their child's behaviour becomes more obvious in the following statement:

No. There was not a big celebration (when he graduated university). It was your job. Their job was to get you through and help you pay for some school. When I was finished school, I was thirty to forty thousand in debt. When my wife finished school, she was a couple thousand in debt. Her parents had already set that all up. It is a different lifestyle. With her parents, they had set aside money for RRSPs, RESPs, everything. They are going to retire, and it is going to be great. For us, our job is to make sure that our parents retire well. So my parents are not only depending on me, but they continue to work really hard. They are building this house. It is all done now, but it is one hundred and three acres of land up north, in Sutton, but they are depending on us to do everything to help them build the house.

Ho grew up in an entrepreneurial household, one where he learned what it took to create and build a successful business. He talks about how his family began running restaurants in a food court.

So there were three restaurants, and that was really interesting. You got to see the logistics, how to do everything, run a business. We had to learn all three of the restaurants. It eventually became four. My mom is a great person, but she is passive-aggressive. She is like, "If you do not work there, then who will?"

The first year I stayed in Bradford, we commuted; we got a Toyota Corolla, and my sister and I drove up to York-dale, because she went to U of T, and we went to school that way. Weekends we would work, days off we would work. We did it for a year. That was the first time my dad took on a business partner, and then he sold because he found out that the business partner was taking money from the business, which is fine, but we made our money in that too, and then we sold it, and my dad took that money that he had from that business and he bought a house in Toronto. So that is when he started the property management bit, using my networks and everything. I rented the houses.

On taking personal responsibility for success and failure:

When things screw up and when things go wrong, you always have to understand that it was your fault, because it is your fault that you did not follow up. It is your fault you didn't go in there and say, "Hey, what is going on?" And you have to learn for next time. That is okay, but if you keep doing the same things wrong over and over again, then that is not good.

A great number of consultants today talk of how businesses and entrepreneurs need to understand the current generation of young adults to provide a workplace where they can thrive. With Ho's traditional thoughts, beliefs, and upbringing, I wondered how he goes about hiring staff for his business.

We hired one of our first employees, and she is still working with us now. She has been amazing. You can tell she comes from a great family; she works really hard. Her parents are still together. She has two sisters and a younger brother. They get it, like unity, making sure you look out for each other, and I guess we lucked out. We got the right person as one of our first hires. She was our first leasing agent. She was so charismatic.

I think the biggest thing that has been lost on this generation is the sense of guilt of disappointment when you have let someone down. My dad was really good at this, and I have learned this now—guilt is a powerful thing. I had to fight for everything. "Oh, I want to go to the movies with my friend." And my dad was like, in his eyes, in his mind, he was like, "Oh I understand, you are going to join a gang." That was how hard it was.

I asked Ho how he would parent his children given what he knows and experienced. I asked if he would use the same techniques as his father, and he reported that he wouldn't.

But, you know what, we have an obligation now because we are educated. We are just given so much more information. So to him (his father) it was like, if you get a tattoo, immediately, you are going to be joining a gang and you are going to be selling drugs on the streets. But for us, we know that sometimes Ace just wants a nose ring because he thought it was cool, and he might get rid of it in a week.

One of the factors I saw that motivated me to write this

book was the changing climate of the young entitled gener-
ation. I asked Ho if he has noticed any changes in the stu-
dents that come to rent properties that his firm manages.

I don't know (why students changed). If there were something wrong with the house, you would never, ever call
your parents. You would call the landlord, and the landlord would probably say go to Home Hardware, pick
something up, and fix it yourself. Back then we didn't
have the internet. So you actually had to look at it, and
say how the heck I am going to fix this. But now, everything, whatever you want, you want to start property
management, Google it. You want to fix a sink, Google
it. How can a group of engineering students not know
how to replace a fluorescent lightbulb? Just Google it.
They will give you step-by-step instructions with video
on how to do it, but they don't do it. Instead they complain to their parents. I think it comes from the fact that
parents might feel guilty that they don't have enough
time because they are working so hard in their careers,
that they give their kids the best they can.

I asked Ho how he has incorporated the lessons he learned
from his parents into his life today.

My parents had the experience of going through war and
the Communist takeover, and so to them it is like you
guys have it made, this is a joke. In Canada when you
work overtime, they don't even kill you, they pay you
time and a half. It is like, get over yourself, work hard
because in Canada, there is no excuse. If you work hard,

you can get somewhere. Even if you are the dumbest person in the world, all you have to do is go to that factory and make sure you hammer that nail into that bumper as hard as you can and do it a million times over, and you are going to provide for your family because all of them have provided for their family doing that.

I asked Ho about leadership and his father.

I look at my dad and I always say he was a leader. Right, he was a leader because he came from Cambodia with my two uncles. Raised them as his own and everything. What is it? It's based on the information you're given at the time to make the best decision for yourself and for your group and adjust and go from there. I think that's, like, my life philosophy. Make the decision based on the best possible information, on the information at that time. From that point on it's just an infinite timeline of adjustments and variability. See what happens. When people fail, it's because they continually fail. It's not just one thing that makes you fail. Sometimes it is, like catastrophic, you can't rule those out. But there's always a turning point, and hopefully, you can make an adjustment and push yourself back up.

More on today's generation, and who is responsible for this change in behaviour:

Yeah, for sure the parents. We have friends who are teachers, and they say the kids are kind of crazy. They don't respect us. That is ludicrous, there's no reason. If there's something wrong and the teacher were to say it to me, I can guarantee you, and you can interview me in ten years, I can guarantee I would take the teacher's side in a second, in a heartbeat. They are the authority, so someone should have said something along the way, "Take off your freaking iPod and just listen to life."

We see this also in housing. Before people would live in student housing, like three or four people, five people, seven people, eight people, and now that rarely ever happens. You can't rent a seven-bedroom house because everybody is so freaking entitled. I want things done my way, I don't want to have to deal with someone else, I don't want to whatever.

So we've moved from five bedrooms, and now I've been saying this for a long time, it should just be one-bedroom units because everybody wants their own thing. They want to do what they freaking want. That's what they're doing, they're just doing bachelor, efficient bachelor fully furnished, fully everything, and they're doing two hundred and fifty of them.

* * *

We complete the interview, and Ho indicates the challenges he faces today with his family and in business. We discuss spanking of his children, and he reports that it may be necessary but infrequently and rarely a tool to use today.

Driving from Waterloo, I am left with the belief that a

number of factors and circumstance influenced Ho's development. The experiences of his mom while she carried him in utero may have had an impact on his temperament and readiness to take on the world to survive from day one.

His father's demonstrated leadership and strong convictions of role and responsibility is also striking. The example of his parents working hard to build a better life for the family, the collective nature of pooling resources is also significant. Growing up, Ho was denied many things and made to work for them. Later, when his parents could afford his requests, he continued to hear the word "no" and was told to work for something if he wanted it. That, to me, appears to be one of the significant parenting strategies that influenced Ho's growth and development into a strong business leader. The discipline within the home was also striking with a sense of obligation for behaviour combined with immediate consequences if those were not met.

8

Kimberly Joines

ACCORDING TO ALPINE Canada, "Kimberly Joines is one of the world's best female sit-skiers. She is a two time IPC world champion, a twenty-two time IPC World Cup Winner, and two-time Paralympic bronze medallist."

She experienced a serious injury that prevented her from competing at the 2010 Vancouver Paralympic Winter Games, an occurrence that tested her character and will to compete. She returned to active competition in 2011. I have a hard time with the "Paralympic" designation. When I watched numerous videos on the sit-ski event, it appears much more daring, dangerous, and in need of skills beyond more "Olympic" events such as the bobsled or luge. I wonder why we can't simply call Kimberly Joines and her team Olympians.

I wanted to interview Kimberly and her parents if possible. I wanted to know how a parent deals with the initial injury that resulted in paralysis and then the continued determination of an adult child who continues to want to push the limits. I interviewed Kimberly, her mother, and grandmother at a coffee shop in Kelowna, British Columbia. Both Kimberly's mom and grandmother are teachers by profession.

What were the rules at home? What were the rules growing up?

There were lots of rules. We're a very rule-orientated family. My dad is Mr. Rules, he is a coach and a phys ed teacher. Very regimented, same lunch every day for thirty-five years.

Kimberly talked about the regime of her father, how he was very into sports and somewhat critical of performance. She reported that her father would often ask questions after games of how she played and what she could do to improve.

Like if this were us after a basketball game and we would go as a family or whatever, for lunch, and then it was like that one play when Billy was here and you were here.

So how did you feel, did you get upset?

I mean, we were so used to that as well, and we wanted to be good athletes, and we were very skilled athletes and wanted to be the best athletes we could. Maybe it was to please him or whatever, but we just got really used to it. I think we butted heads more as adults because taking that more matter of fact, but as a kid he was always right with whatever he was doing with the salt and pepper shakers. Like you could tell him, no, it didn't happen that way, and he would find game footage to prove to you it did. He was hard, very critical.

(The difference between being a parent who is encouraging and tough, and one who crosses the line is difficult to understand or measure. Parents do what they believe to be the best for their children. Kimberly learned many things from her father that continued to permeate our discussion.)

Kimberly's mother continued:

Mother: If they played a game, he didn't concentrate on the positives, like, that was a really good throw or that was a really good catch. He would look to improve them. That's why he was doing it, out of love. Playing his teacher role.

Mother: He wanted them to be better and in his mind, as a teacher and a coach, that was how he looked at them in any sport.

Kimberly: It's the only thing he knows how to do. It's the only way he knows how to communicate, is to do it through instruction. It trained me to be an exceptional athlete. He was meant to raise an Olympian, and he did.

Mother: Sometimes it was too much.

I asked Kimberly's mom what her life was like the nine months prenatally.

Normal, very normal.

Any stress or tension?

No, I had Shane (sibling) at home already, and I lived in a very small community.

Very young parents.

I was twenty-one when I had her, and I was nineteen when I had Shane.

No stresses?

Not really.

If any anxiety, it would be from having Shane, being in that situation pre-marriage, and if anything's going to cause stress, that would have been it.

Kimberly: And my brother does have ADHD.

You wouldn't have any yourself?

Kimberly: Depression issues.

No ADHD?

I guess, potentially, I was debating that actually just last week, if I maybe am somewhat not properly diagnosed.

Have you ever been concussed before?

Yes.

How many times?

Not seriously, like, not on blackout very many times but seriously three times.

Early though? Early years?

Not early years, it was with skiing later.

Any concussions in your family?

Mother: And with your brother later. I didn't have any.

Kimberly: Dad probably had some through sports.

Mother: I don't think so. He always played basketball and soccer.

Grandmother: He is from a family, though, of athletes.

Mother: His brothers, but they didn't play hockey, football so that's when you get concussions.

Kimberly: I think, although the way I was raised by dad, is this athlete gave me a lot of positive characteristics, like the hardworking and the problem-solving.

So what did you watch growing up as far as work ethic? What did you see?

Kimberly: I watched his personal discipline as well. You would hear all his stories because he would coach every team at the school he worked at. He was coaching all the time, and you definitely learned, you know, you never missed a practice without making sure you got a hold of your coach. Little things like that, some athletes never realize that's an important part of being an athlete.

Mother: And time management because you're playing different sports and just organizing your time.

Kimberly: Making sure you don't accidentally miss a game because you have three soccer games today in different locations.

So outside of sports did you have to work?

Mother: No.

Kimberly: I did work.

Mother: But this was my input as a mom, is I would rather them play sports in high school than be working.

What if they hadn't wanted to play sports?

Kimberly: Probably would have had to work.

Mother: They were born to play sports.

Mother: But I always said that I would rather them play high school sports than work.

Kimberly: I was always really thrifty and I always had savings. Like, I got annoyed that I couldn't start my RRSP when I was nine, because the bank's like, you don't have a real job, you can't start one. But that, again, is also my dad's Mr. Be Prepared For the Future and Have A Real Job.

Mother: The working does interfere with children playing sports. They do, because if they have to work, and I didn't want my kids to have to make that choice.

Kimberly: I mostly babysat, and I delivered papers.

How were you disciplined? I get the sense that you might have been disciplined a few times growing up?

Oh yeah. I was also very bad.

Go to your bedroom?

Well, no, Dad gave me some good spankings.

And if I had children right now I would spank them because I deserved every spanking I ever got.

Did you get a lot of them?

No, maybe like six spankings.

Grandmother: I don't ever remember her getting spanked.

I would do something wrong, like the one time I pranked called 911 for example, and they called back and I'm in the kitchen…got spanked for that one.

How old were you?

Eight, grade three. I would say probably ten times I was spanked in my childhood that I can remember, the thing I did that fully warranted the discipline, I got.

How were your grades?

Top-notch.

Did you work hard?

Yes.

Mother: She worked really hard.

Kimberly: My brother got good marks without trying hard. I had to try very hard for it. It was I think difficult for them to discipline us a lot of the time because it's like, I am the star athlete of all my teams and getting straight As in school, but then I'm being a jerk on the school trip and getting sent home and suspended.

Were you expected to get good grades?

Kimberly: Yeah.

Mother: She worked harder than our expectations. Like for us eighty percent is wonderful, that would have been enough. But she had to go for the ninety-six percent, and sometimes kill herself doing it, like studying after playing sports all day, and I didn't put that into her. But for me, seventy-five, eighty that's enough effort, but she had to get the ninety-six.

Grandmother: Mom and Dad are completely different here, and you got to feel it.

Kimberly: I think he was good as long as our sports…

You guys are a lot alike?

Mother: I remember many drives home from games…

You get from high school and then what do you do?

I immediately moved to the mountains to be a snowboard bum.

Wouldn't your parents freak out and want you to go to university?

Kimberly: No. They knew I was going to go at some point.

Grandmother: But you were doing that in between where they go work the ski hill.

Kimberly: There was certainly the expectation that we were to go to university. They knew we would do it, so they didn't pressure us in a particular time frame.

Mother: I think kids need that after high school, and I do more so now. But these kids, it's so intense in high school, more so now, even than when Kim went. But they need a break. These parents that freak out because their children are not going to university right after high school, it's like, give them a break. They need time to explore, get to know themselves. For these kids that take time off school and work, or travel the world, I think that is a really positive thing.

So did you get a cheque from mom and dad every month?

No, I mean generally anything we wanted that was—like, we always had what we needed, and we got to play whatever sports or if we wanted to pick up an instrument, they would pay for those sorts of things, but anything we wanted that was frivolous it was, you save your money, buy it yourself.

Anything outside of school you had to earn yourself?

Yeah, and if we were living at home—what it turned into eventually is, if you were living at home and not in school, Dad made us pay rent.

Is that old-fashioned or smart?

Mother: I think it's teaching them to be responsible.

Kimberly: We always knew the value of a dollar.

Grandmother: Things have really changed now.

Mother: I don't like the way things have changed.

Grandmother: I don't either.

Do think that's because parents are wimps?

Mother: They are, they're afraid to stand up to their kids. They want their kids to like them, they don't want to disappoint their kids.

Grandmother: They've got high expectations.

Kimberly: It's like less along of the line of like you should respect your parents, that's how we were raised. Dad's number one thing would be truth and respect. Mutual respect, and it goes with a coaching relationship too, he parented that.

Grandmother: But kids have a harder time getting jobs nowadays, you have to be much more educated.

Mother: They don't have the drive. Children nowadays expect those jobs to be served to them on a silver platter.

If you don't have any money though, you're hungry though. If you need to eat, to pay rent or something, you find a way.

Grandmother: Yeah, if you have boys and you want the wheels, you work for it. Well, we didn't buy the wheels, but now parents buy the wheels.

Mother: They want the best now days.

Grandmother: We bought a beater for three hundred.

Mother: Even houses. I look at these houses that some of these young people are buying and think, wow, they must be in debt or mom and dad must be paying the mortgage for them. The expectations are out of control.

Grandmother: I don't know what's happened, really.

Kimberly: And I find like using this comparison, so my dad's remarried, and his wife has two children. They grew up in a divorced home, like with a mom working three jobs to get them through school and stuff. So they grew up probably always wanting things. Shane and I never grew up wanting things, we're very middle income, not spoiled in any way, but not wanting. Neither he nor I care about material possessions at all, like now I live in a miner shack in the mountains and he's living about.

Grandmother: He's thirty-six and renting a bedroom in a house.

Kimberly: But he's travelled to more places than most and that sort of thing.

How old were you when your parents divorced?

Twenty-four.

How did you feel about that?

Kimberly: It messed with us a little bit. It was out of blue and unexpected.

Grandmother: It messed with all of us.

Mother: All divorces do.

Kimberly: It was weird as an adult because you maybe shouldn't care about it in the same way, like we did, and then my brother was like, I'm out of here, and went to Sweden for a year to, like, avoid the situation, and I was the go between parents.

Can we talk a little bit about March?

About my injury?

Yeah.

Oh yeah. That shit doesn't bother me at all.

I just watched the video over again, and I want to talk a little bit about that day. How do you feel about it?

Kimberly: I mean, yeah, you've seen the story, but I was just pushing my limits every day on the snowboard. Pushed them wrong the one day. I think it was always one of the first comments out of my mom's mouth, I don't know if she remembers. I guess when they called her and told her about it she's like, I guess it's only a matter of time. Because I was always in the hospital.

Mother: Always broken bones, always in the hospital. In the end it was like I would just drop her off, and phone me when you're ready, honey.

Kimberly: In grade four, she sent me in a cab to deal with my broken arm at the next town over.

Mother: And even when I went when she broke her back, and they phone me from the hospital, and I was about to join her in Lake Louise and do some skiing because it was my spring break. And they phoned me from the hospital, and I totally wasn't prepared for the seriousness of it because they don't tell you on the phone. I was so used to another injury, what now? So I get in my car, and it was of course a lot more serious then what they let you know on the phone.

Did you say in a video that you got the best out of your legs that you could have or something?

Totally, yeah. I said I used my legs more than the average person did when I was eighteen, nineteen. There's not a sport I didn't try. So at least I wasn't sitting on the couch most of my childhood. I know that happens, and then you have all this regret about what you've missed the opportunity to do. Whereas I don't feel I have any of that regret. Like, it's unfortunate this is going to be the rest of the time, because there's a lot of other cool things I probably could have done, but by no means did I waste my time.

Mother: She's always had the most amazing attitude, and even in the hospital with the splints still on her neck, she's saying, well now maybe I can get a Paralympic award.

As a parent how did you support that?

Mother: Kimberly made it easier for us because of her attitude. Because you know a lot of people that injure themselves become dark, and they give up.

Grandmother: Wimpish.

Mother: They don't look at the future as being a new world for them, which Kim did. Even lying in that bed, she's thinking I can still do it, but I can do it in a different manner. Like she's, had them of course, dark days but...

Kimberly: I just knew that numbers wise that my chances to succeed in the Paralympic side was going to be the best or better.

You were already figuring this out in the hospital?

Mother: Yes.

Before surgery.

Mother: She had that all figured out.

Grandmother: But you weren't sure which sport because you did basketball first, but you weren't as good in basketball. When she was in the hospital, I remember she had already planned on the vehicle she was going to have made.

Kimberly: I made sure I got my license right away.

Grandmother: She had ordered a vehicle already.

Some people think you're supposed to grieve and all this stuff, but it sounds like...

I never did.

Grandmother: She got really active.

I'm closer to grieving now than I ever was then. It was easier to fixate and focus on like a new thing, a new task, but because of that, all the people that worked with me at the hospital were just like waiting for the crash.

Everybody's different.

And it never came, and now after many years of being beat down with my skiing career, I'm in a lot a tougher place than I ever was because that was the first of many, but the shit-kickings I've had since have been way harder for me.

Falls, you mean?

Oh yeah, just the breaking...

Did you have to learn all over again?

Yeah, and I'm still learning it. Like sit-skiing's harder than, like, I skied and snowboarded and now I sit-ski, and sit-ski is way more difficult. Like tight trees, there's just a lot of additional problems, like I can't just free ski around the hill by myself. My boyfriend follows behind to make sure if I fall in a tree hill that he, like, clears the snow out of my face because my arms are stuck down here.

So you as a parent don't worry?

Mother: Well, I stopped worrying because it's out of my control.

When did you stop worrying?

Mother: And just going back when you talked about as a shrink when we went through the Glenrose for three months and there's a team of people, like nutritionist, physio, pysch dude, and that was my question because Kim was always so positive all the time, and I was worried when is going to happen. Like, when is it going to drop out, when is she going to bottom out. And they said exactly what you said, sometimes it doesn't happen. And in Kim's case, like she says right now, starting to grieve the fact that her career might be over, and that's where she's starting to…

That would bum you out, anyway. This whole thing waiting to happen, I don't know if it's true, we're all different.

Mother: But with the worry thing. I worried a lot when Kim was skiing because they were going down that mountain at eighty kilometres per hour, even though she's got her helmet. And she goes, she says it's either first or into the fence. That's her attitude, podium or fence. So Kim gives it one hundred and ten percent, and that's really fast down the mountain, and so I did worry. But then, after a while, you think, well you know, you can get killed crossing the street, you know. You can get killed in different ways, and for Kimberly, she's doing something she loves to do, it's her passion. It doesn't help me to worry because I have no control over it. So worrying to me is just—of course, I still have it—but I don't dwell on it because what's the point. She's going to do what she loves to do.

Kimberly: They were certainly never happy when they got the phone call and I was like on the road. If I ever called, it wasn't for like a chat, it was because I was in the hospital.

Grandmother: It's another break. What part of the body is it this time?

Kimberly: And, like, two years ago, I busted both of my shoulders in Russia and spent a week in a Russian hospital. No arms, being spoon-fed by a bunch of nurses, but like, literally, couldn't even touch my face to scratch it.

This is unfortunate, when you get injured, it's just part of a sport. Is there a bit of a rush with that? It's another thing to overcome?

Kimberly: I guess, yeah. Hopefully, I don't thrive on that.

Mother: Adrenaline junky, kind of going for that.

Kimberly: I don't think that that's part of it, I don't know. For me I've always hurt myself a lot whether I just have more breakable bones...

Mother: Bad karma, she says.

Kimberly: Bad karma, bad luck. I don't know what it is. But because I've been in this sport a long time and I know a lot of sit-skiers. There's a few others that have had rocky careers like mine with a lot of injuries but more generally than just everybody.

How did you handle the word "no" growing up? If your parents said no, you can't do it.

I mean usually we only heard the word "no" when it was truly like, you're not to do that. So it wasn't really like an option.

What if someone told you weren't good enough or you weren't going to do it.

I would prove them wrong. Like, if someone had told me this jump you're about to make, you're going to break your back, so maybe don't do the jump. I would be like, no, I'm going to do it, but I'm just not going to break my back.

Mother: And Kim wanted to be better than the boys. Keep up with the boys. Not just girls, she had already kind of blown the girl business out of the water. She was athlete of the year at St. Francis Xavier in Edmonton.

What did you do?

Kimberly: My high school.

Mother: In high school. That was a very big high school, and she was athlete of the year. So that tells you how good she was at what she did.

Kimberly: And it was funny, too, because the tradition at our school is that the athlete of the year from the previous year presents the award to the next year's recipient. So I won it one year, and then I presented it the next year from a wheelchair.

All this happened after your injury?

Mother: Right away.

Kimberly: So at the school's banquet all these people are like, what happened? All the previous athletes were like, oh my god, I couldn't imagine what you were going through, because they're athletes and they couldn't imagine. And you're like, it really wasn't a thing, I don't know. I saw a lot of people way worse off than me.

Mother: I think at Glenrose, too, for us, Kimberly was still Kimberly, and she doesn't have her legs, but she's still my daughter whom I'm going to love and have conversations with, and she's still Kimberly. Whereas at Glenrose, when you do see the brain injury people, they've lost their people. It was a different world, and I think just being at Glenrose for those three months, it helped me to see that, yes, Kimberly—it's a serious disability, but there's worse, and I think that helped to.

Mother: I know she always needs that "you are great." She wants the gold.

Kimberly: It's always that, it's never good enough.

Mother: For her, not us.

Kimberly: And Dad. It was like years of succeeding, period. Like, what can we do that's better. So it's like, okay, I never got to win an Olympic gold medal and now my career is probably over, so no opportunity.

Kimberly: My shoulders are broken, I need two surgeries. Even my dad is glad it's over.

Grandmother: She's got opportunities to use this (pointing to her brain). That she's got a hell of a lot, and this is where she is going to do her next reaching for the moon.

So what's the next then?

Kimberly: I don't know yet, it's still very transitional. I started working for one of my sponsors that's been with me for a lot of years. We'll see if it turns into more work.

Mother: I think she could write a book.

Kimberly: Well, I have lots of writing. I just don't know what form it will take yet. I've written many chapters.

Grandmother: She has a degree too, she could use her degree.

Kimberly: I have a Bachelor of Commerce.

Grandmother: And she got that in between.

Mother: She's a very good writer, both my kids. I have such talented, skillful kids, and not just their brains are bright. They're artistic, they can write, like, amazing. They're both very athletic.

Kimberly: I'm more driven then my brother. Like, all else, we're very similar, but I've always been more focused and driven, and that's why…

So tell me about the stigma that you're a Paralympic athlete.

With my sport in being on the para side you mean?

A little bit. For sure we're looked at as inferior, no matter how hard I try. But even me, the way I approached it and really is like I said, I was like numbers-wise, I'm going to have a lot more chances to succeed on the para side. And it's true. If you're an athlete and you hurt yourself, you can pick a sport. Pick a sport, and you can go to play that.

Mother: And some of her friends are in two para sports.

On others trying her sport:

We love when someone tries it. Like occasionally, whenever a coach is willing to get in the sit-ski but very rarely. And these are people that should try it, they're coaches, they're trying to tell us do this, do that.

They don't sit-ski?

No.

Too scary?

Kimberly: It is, you're just so vulnerable. So for us, when you crash, you tuck your arms in, and like, usually breaking bones or whatever. But people who aren't used to it, they want to put their arms out and stuff, and that's just like, oh yay, they're just going to break their shoulders.

Mother: When they crash, it's bucket over, bucket over. It's terrible crashes.

Kimberly: The only person I'm in contact with from the team right now is our sports psych, and he's a pysch that I get along with very well. So we have lots of conversations and stuff. And it's like I definitely more like mourning the loss of it and trying to find my value in the world.

Grandmother: It's bad, bad, bad right now.

Kimberly: I didn't think I would be one of those athletes that would have trouble in retirement, but I'm coming to realize that I'm probably the most atypical person that's going to have problems with it, because my entire life was really focused on that and achieving. So until I find something that I'm as passionate about and that is challenging in the same way, I'm probably going to be floating in and out.

Mother: Yeah, seeking.

Kimberly: But I'm not yet looking back and just being proud of the career that I had.

Mother: She's not there yet, but she will be.

Kimberly: Just because there was stuff I wanted to—I wish I wanted to end on a better note. I went to World Champs and did not finish both my races, which I almost never do, but it was like my last big event, and I just like botched it and fell right out of the gate both times. But I was so fried and burnt out by the time that happened and destroyed my shoulders in January but was still skiing with them in March, not realizing that I needed two surgeries.

Mother: Shouldn't have done that.

Kimberly: Should have stopped.

Mother: Your sports team should have stopped you.

Grandmother: Yeah, but why do athletes do it? I mean it's always happening. Hockey players play, they should have quit when they were on a high. They don't.

Mother: Well, boxers with these concussions. Yeah, but Kim still had those achievements she wanted to reach.

Kimberly: Some of my skiing was the best it had ever been. Like in Slalom, I've never skied slalom that well.

Mother: Well, because you cut out that one event.

Kimberly: I cut out the downhill. And then got hurt by the ski lift last year.

Where are you spiritually?

Closer to atheist than anything. I was raised Catholic but by no means overly churchy.

Still doing cardio?

Kimberly: I can't. My shoulders cannot do any sort of exercise.

Grandmother: That's another thing, she can't exercise, and that's difficult.

Kimberly: But I can't yet.

Grandmother: Because she needs the strength.

Kimberly: I have a surgeon consult next week.

You got a good shoulder guy?

Yeah, the best.

Are they going to replace them?

No, do patch repair, which is more than my dad can say. It's just the replacement only lasts for fifteen years, so I'm so young that they don't want to put one in so young. It may be something down the road.

Do you have a lot of pain?

Mother: Yes.

Kimberly: Oh yeah. Like I literally can't lift a couple pounds, like really screwed right now. There's zero option and I would be able to like free ski, that's what I always loved. I only raced because it was a way to get paid for skiing. But racing wasn't my love, it was powder. So I want to go back to that, but my shoulders are too screwed to do that right now or any exercise.

So what's parenting like when she's at this stage in her life? How do you parent her now, if there is such a thing?

Mother: I know, but I am still going to listen and I am so supportive. Like my whole thing, I just want my child happy and healthy. That's what most parents want. And Kim's neither right now.

Grandmother: I don't worry about her at all. I don't really worry about her. There's only a couple reasons why you need your shoulders. Recreational, you need your arms because that's how you get around, so it will make life much easier and get out of pain.

Kimberly: And I am a person that needs to exercise to…

Grandmother: Well, you can't get overweight too, darling.

Kimberly: Oh, and in a chair it's super easier.

Kimberly: So I have some movement already. I can walk with leg braces, except you need your shoulders for that. But it's not practical for getting around, and it's way too soon. For me, honestly, being in the chair doesn't bother me at all, so I really have no need for devices to change my state of being.

So how would you parent if you had a little person?

I would be a hard-ass. Honestly, I know that it's one of

the reasons I'm planning not to have children because I think I would be so tough.

Grandmother: Like you were, like you were.

Mother: And she sees a lot of her friends parenting.

Like by today's standards, or your standards?

Yup, by today's. I would be very similar to how my dad parented me.

And like I said, I deserved every one of the spankings I did get, because I did a lot of bad stuff. I was also testing those boundaries as well, and I think they were actually quite casual with us. Like my brother and me were both, although we both got great marks, great athletes, all that, we were bad kids, we did some bad stuff. And you know, they were pretty chill about it.

Oh yeah, if we were ever drunk at a party, all that time they would say, we'll come get you.

How did you, as an involved grandmother, deal with all her accomplishments and barriers?

Grandmother: I was very proud of her. We always wish she would have quit.

When did you wish?

Grandmother: Probably when you got your best medal, wherever that was.

Kimberly: But you never know it's going to be the best one.

Grandmother: The most disappointing one was Vancouver.

Kimberly: No, I know. I broke.

Grandmother: What three weeks before?

Kimberly: Yeah, the opening ceremonies at the Olympics, I broke my hip. So the guy who owns this coffee shop, I fell leaving his house in the corner.

Grandmother: I thought you fell at the doctor's office.

Kimberly: I was staying at Dustin's house and we had coffee from this kind of establishment here, and I put down the coffees and just went to wheel backward, I thought he (my boyfriend) was behind me to support me down the stairs, he wasn't. I fell down two steps. Broke my hip, knew I broke it immediately. Hit the ground, was like, no.

Grandmother: There's the end of the games.

Kimberly: Immediate pain, like I do feel below my level of injury. I knew it was broken and opening ceremonies of the Olympics just flashed in my head. I'm like, I'm out, I'm out.

So what did you do?

Grandmother: She went anyway.

Kimberly: Well, I went because... I was nursing a broken hip, there was no way I was going to ski, but our team would have lost a staff member if we were one athlete less, so I went and went to the athlete's village and watched my friends compete.

Grandmother: And you came on at the end, you were on at the end.

Did you get a pin in, or did they just leave it rest?

Kimberly: No, a pin, which I've had removed, but my hip is still ten degrees off of what it should be, so it…

Grandmother: That was probably the saddest thing, because that was the one you were…

Kimberly: It was the biggest heartbreak.

Grandmother: You were home, and you were at your peak, practically.

Kimberly: No, I was destined to win a lot of stuff, and then I didn't. Before Sochi, I broke both my shoulders.

What about self-doubt? How do you handle self-doubt?

Kimberly: I don't think I doubt myself that much. Like right now, I'm only doubting myself because I see myself being weaker than I should be, or weaker than what I know I am. So I'm not being true to my real self right now, but that is because my psychologist is trying to get me to process a lot of those past traumas, and so I'm more emotional.

Grandmother: She's having trouble believing she's human.

Kimberly: It's hard for me to be emotional.

What does that mean?

Grandmother: I don't know, just that she can't do everything she tries.

Kimberly: And I've been very good and being very strong and just, like, not focusing on anything bad.

Mother: And she's been confident since she was a little kid, because by kindergarten she wanted to have sleepovers at other people's houses. I always think little kindergarten kids are clinging to their moms, and my son didn't want to go to camp, didn't want to go to any sleepovers because he wanted to stay home. Whereas Kim in kindergarten is like, can I go and sleep over at my friend's?

Kimberly: I was always independent.

Mother: Kim liked that, she was happy to leave the house for a week and go to camp and sleep over.

Grandmother: Your dad worked with you independently. Remember when he used to make you do all sorts of gymnastic crap when you're just a little thing. He did, and I don't ever remember him doing that with Shane.

Mother: She's always been a risk-taker, always. Her brother was more I'm going to watch, I'm going to see what other people do it, and then I'll try it. Where Kim has to be the first one to do it, that's her whole life.

Grandmother: And that's how she broke so many bones.

Kimberly: It was more fun competing with the boys as a girl though, like there were a few guys that I've reconnected with since that were, like, roommates at Lake Louise or whatever. And they're like, man, you always showed us up. Like, there's one cliff that you drop at Lake Louise, it's called the Man Maker Corners. Because you can't see what you're jumping into and everyone tumbles on their landing. So I'm sitting at the top with like three other guys, the rest of our posse already has dropped it, and this is a bunch of first years sitting there. And it's like, well, guess I'm up and jump off it, and the guys are like, shit now you got to do it because Kim did it.

What tips or advice would you give for a parent who wanted to raise a strong leader?

I think definitely encouraging independence and they have to learn their own lessons. You can't learn a lesson by being told it, and even my dad has improved over the years, that realizing that like him telling us not to do something isn't going to make us not to do it. We need to learn from our mistakes, and I think my brother and I both did a lot of that, which is why we would be disciplined severely because you also learned your limits.

You consider yourself a strong leader?

I do, yeah.

When did you realize it?

Kimberly: Always, like, I always was the ringleader. I was always a bad influence on my friends.

Mother: Because she was a risk-taker.

Kimberly: In school if we were doing projects and stuff, I was always going to be the person with all the ideas, and to a fault. I always have a comment and am not always accepting enough of other people's opinions, because I always think mine is the best.

Well, if you know you are right, why would you bother wasting time?

Definitely some of that and some of sport, although the characteristics that make me a great athlete, they also make you neurotic and obsessed to a fault. But I think kids need to learn from their mistakes.

So when are you going to tell Canadians you're retiring?

Well, I need to ride injury status for a little while longer, so we'll see how the surgeon consults go and what time frame we're looking at for recovery. Potentially in the spring, but depending on my shoulders.

What advice would you give a pregnant woman or someone who is going to adopt today with a new baby about how to discipline and raise them?

Mother: Well, it's got to be right for you. Everybody has

different parenting styles, and it all comes from their background and how they were parented. So that's one thing, don't judge yourself on what other people are doing, because it's got to be right for you, and I may look at young mothers and say I wouldn't be doing that, but if it works for them. You can't force people to be a certain type of parent, like, it's not in their...

But aren't there certain things right and wrong—

Mother: Like certainly as a teacher right now with seven-year-olds, discipline is good, and the kids will come to me, when you said that they are not used to "no" and that's it exactly. I'll get seven-year-old kids coming and arguing with me as a teacher, they're arguing with me. And I tell them, there's no negotiation, I said no, but they're not used to that. But they learn that I'm not negotiating here, I mean no. But I have to work with the kids because at home, exactly no is *not* no. So they're told no like six or seven times before the parents give up because they're too tired, or they'd just rather go onto something else and it's easier to give in. I always think parents that say no, that's the brave thing, because that's the one that takes more effort to make their kids stop what they're doing.

So why don't you think parents have more courage?

Kimberly: I think parents are overworked, I think parents are tired. I think parents are so tuned into their technology that they would rather be texting to a friend rather than dealing with what's happening with their children. I think parents would rather have their kids be quiet doing their thing, and saying no takes more energy.

Grandmother: I think they don't want to say no, I think they feel they're going to lose their love if they don't say yes. If they're going to carry the screaming kid out of Safeway and not say, if you're not quiet, I'm going to take you out.

Kimberly: I think people also really need to lead by example. So for me, most of the characteristics I picked by watching how my dad approached his sport or hearing him talk to the teams he was coaching, and so you learn what is right and wrong. My friends, all in this mountain town I live in, like one set of friends of ours, they all mountain bike as a family all the time, they're like, mountain biking saved our family, it saved our marriage. Because all of a sudden, it's this thing they're all doing together. But I think that's really important because like you said, a parent just sitting there on technology and in the same room, but not socializing. These guys are going spending seven hours in the day mountain biking together. Shows the children how to be, how to be involved and be a part of life, that makes it excited.

Grandmother: I think they're still afraid. I think they're afraid if they say no they're doing the wrong thing. I think they worry too much about raising their children nowadays.

Kimberly: And they don't want the kid mad at them ever, which is silly.

Mother: I laugh when the parents do threats too, like if

you don't stop crying, I'm going to make you sit in the car. That part bothers me a lot. I'm all about if you say something with our kids, we carry through. And sometimes we made threats that we have to carry through now, but we did. Like any time we said, this is what's going to happen, then we did it, and nowadays, I don't see that happening.

What advice would you give to a woman who is having a baby, or a guy, what would be your parenting advice? As far as discipline.

Mother: I don't know, every baby, every kid, is different.

Grandmother: You can't have these set rules, like quiet corner I thought, was an excellent thing that came out. Fifteen years ago.

* * *

From the information provided in the interview, I wondered about the following:

1. Kimberly demonstrated oppositional behaviour growing up that appeared to have been harnessed by the combination of her mother and father's parenting styles.

2. Sports were an outlet for her, helping her cope with the usual challenges of being a teenager, and then after her spinal cord injury continued to be her focus.

3. Kimberly feels that her father's support, structure, and, at times thought to be critical, appraisal of her athletic performances continued to push her to higher levels of achievement. She reported that the discipline he provided was instrumental in her success.

4. She hates to lose, never quits, and will participate in athletics "hurt" until she is unable to continue. The desire and will to win appears to have been witnessed by watching her parents and grandmother growing up.

5. Early on in life, Kimberly considered herself to be a strong leader in school, being the captain on most sport teams, and also leadership may have been demonstrated by leading her peers into more negative types of behaviour. As an international athlete, she leads by example with limited fanfare, a common trait of the six leaders interviewed for this book. (I should have been clear… I also lead in positive ways… group leader in school projects, captain of all of my teams growing up, etc.)

6. Her strong will and determination are now deeply ingrained in her character—with integrity and confidence for her future challenges. Her parents and extended family providing her with a strong sense of unconditional love and support built her confidence and self-esteem.

9

John Milne

JOHN MILNE IS a sixty-year-old retired secondary school teacher and administrator. At the University of Western Ontario, John was a vital member of the varsity football team, winning National Championships in 1974, 1976, and 1977. He was a starting offensive lineman as a freshman until his final game as a senior. John led the team with his quiet sense of dedication, example, and strong work ethic.

I first met John in 1975 when I was a freshman defensive lineman and had to practice against John, where he pretty much beat me up in drills on a daily basis. He was very strong, with quick feet, and a heart that would never quit. He wasn't a talker when he played, nor cheerleader, but let his play do the talking for him. As an all-star offensive tackle he was one of the main reasons Western was so dominant in college football during that time.

When he finished playing at Western, John became a teacher in Waterloo, Ontario, initially in elementary school and then as a secondary school special education teacher and football coach. He and his family then moved back to London, Ontario, where he taught special education at the secondary school level. He later took on additional responsibility becoming a department head.

He spent the last eight years of his career as a high school vice principal until a few years ago, when he retired. John was a leader on the field, playing university football, in his chosen profession of education, and then, as a father, he demonstrated his dedication to his family. When his marriage didn't work out, he chose to dedicate his time to work, to provide for his family and raise his three daughters. He chose to neglect his personal wants and needs until the youngest daughter was established as an adult. It is this leadership as a father and dedication to his obligation as a parent that is an example to all men and requires that his story be told in this book. How did John become the leader that he is, living his life with integrity, honouring his obligation to his family, and dedication to his faith and beliefs?

I interviewed John in London, Ontario. John began by explaining his early childhood, what he witnessed with his parents, and what he learned from them.

What did your dad do? What was his job?

My dad worked in a factory. He was a millwright, which was an industrial mechanic.

108

And your mom worked at home?

She was a nurse. Well, she was at home until we were all in school. I was the youngest of three, so I was in elementary school when she started to work outside the home. She was a nurse who worked part-time at a nursing home, and then when I was in, probably grade seven or eight, she went back to work full-time at St. Mary's Hospital here in London and then worked there until retirement.

Did you see a lot of hard work growing up?

Oh yeah, my dad's family. He was from a family of ten, they grew up on a farm.

Ten family members on a farm?

Yes. He was the second oldest, so he took over the farm when he got older with his older brother. So he was very good with his hands.

And that was before you came along?

Oh yeah.

So he's grinding it, mom's grinding it. What was discipline like when you were a kid?

Well, it was always "wait until your dad gets home." I had two older sisters, and I was usually the one that was getting in trouble for whatever happened. My dad would spank me with his bare hand.

You knew what the rules were, or no?

Oh yeah. You knew what you could get away with and what you couldn't.

John talked about hearing the word "no" quite a bit growing up. Do you think it was because they couldn't, or they knew it wasn't good for you?

I think it was a combination of the two. They grew up through the Depression, so they didn't see a lot of extras, so they probably didn't understand why. I remember one thing that's vivid with me is, I played football in high school. In grade ten or eleven, I wanted to get some cleats because that would be good. I didn't get them because my dad didn't see that there was any need for them.

The other ones were fine?

I had running shoes, so why do you need cleats.

So you think it was they couldn't, like a lot of our parents, or do you think it's just they figured out you shouldn't get everything you want?

I think they had that figured out because, again from their experience I guess, they didn't have everything. What they didn't hold back on, I guess you might find this funny, but we were always well-fed. Food wasn't an issue, education wasn't an issue, if you had to spent money on something related to school, but we didn't have the toys that kids today have. Or you know if you had a bike, you had one bike and it lasted you.

Did you have to work?

No, I started working probably in grade eleven at a grocery store, but that wasn't a push.

Did it on your own?

Yeah.

Went to school. Grades were good?

No, I wasn't a good student. In high school I tended to be more concerned about sports or whatever.

So then you get to university. What was that like? Were you one of those highly-recruited players?

Well, I remember several members of our team went up to Western, probably our coach set up the meeting with Frank Cosentino, and he met us as a group. And then he introduced us to John Metras, we walked around a little bit around Thames Hall or something, I guess, pretty foggy memory. But I remember doing that and then tried out with the other like one hundred and forty people.

Were there any kinks against you? Anything going against you?

Oh yeah, my size, my weight.

What was your size and weight? Not in the program, but in real life.

I'm always struggling with what my height is. Probably in first year I weighed two twenty-five, I guess.

Well even then, it's pretty good. That was good, you're quick. What were they looking for do you think back then?

I remember the first night of football training camp in 1974, Joe, a high school teammate, and I standing up in front of the veterans, and they asked me how fast I was. And the way I guess I react to questions like that is, I said I was lightning fast. My nickname was born! From that night to this day, I am called Lightning.

I heard this story a few times from other guys.

Yes, and that was the captain who said that. So wasn't particularly fast, but I was strong. I lifted weights at the start of grade eleven.

Did you have a chip on your shoulder do you think?

I think so, probably.

Self-induced or a lot of people telling you that you couldn't be successful?

I would say that a few people said I was too small to go out for football.

What did your high school coach say?

I think they were supportive.

Parents, what were they saying?

They were neither here or there. It didn't mean too much to them.

Do you think their philosophy was you provide, obviously because they came from the Depression, so giving people a place to live and food was important for your kids and was the whole quality time thing a big deal back then when you were growing up with your folks?

Well, we never really went on many vacations. That was a rarity, or if it was, we had to be back Sunday to go to church. So it was two or three-day vacation, it wasn't anywhere like a week or anything longer like that. So quality time, I don't think there was a lot of vacation time. You know if my dad was on holidays, he was painting the house or doing stuff.

So when you get to university, you played your freshman year? Was that a surprise to you?

It was a surprise I guess. In training camp, every day you go to look at the board to see if your name is on there and you're cut, so you don't have to go to the next practice.

How much do you think is physical and how much is heart do you think? To play your position? The way you played it.

Just throwing numbers out, but I would say if you didn't have that heart or desire, that would have to be like seventy-five or eighty percent because everybody can have the physical part. You can spend your time in the weight room or whatever. And we all saw that, guys who were physical, but they didn't have the head or the heart.

Would you get frustrated when some of those guys were on the team and they didn't do anything and still sort of hung around because they had so much talent? Because everybody has those guys.

Not really, because if you were starting, you had a different mission. The guys that weren't starting, they could do whatever they wanted during practice I guess.

So that first college bowl, I was pressing grapes in my dad's basement, listening to it on CBC when you guys were coming back in the beginning. You played and then you got injured, because I remember they were talking about that on the radio. I was still in high school. How did you handle that day?

Yeah, that was about two minutes left in the third quarter and our fullback was coming through the line, and his helmet met my knee. I'd never been injured before, so it was weird. I remember when Dr. Kennedy came out, and I pointed to the other knee, I was in so much pain I didn't know. But I remember the captain coming to talk me and he says, we'll get that ring for you.

So when did you start feeling like you were a leader yourself, because we all kind of knew it differently. But when did you start feeling like a leader on the team?

I don't know if I did feel like a leader.

Well, you led through example, through hard work, through what you do in the offseason. You just did it?

Yeah, it was just your job.

Would you say you were a grinder?

Oh yeah, in that position, offensive line, you don't get much recognition, so your pride comes in the fact that you know that you gained ten yards or the pass was completed or whatever. It's not like you made the tackle, you don't hear your name on the loud speaker, that so-and-so blocked for the running back.

John finishes at Western then starts teaching with the final eight years being in administration. As a vice principal, he was required to deal with discipline issues at his high schools.

I asked him if he saw a change in teenagers while he was taking care of those schools.

Oh, most definitely.

Where do you think the changes are?

I think the change comes with entitlement. They feel they're supposed to be given things and not earn them.

Did you see it in coaching too?

Oh yeah. Well, what I saw in coaching was there was a lack of commitment, or probably even worse now, with the different opportunities kids have or whatever. But what I found, which was frustrating, is you'd look around and at a Monday practice, there would be ten guys missing. You couldn't get consistency because whatever they were doing, it was more important than what you were doing. So that was difficult because you can't really build much on it.

And you can't discipline, or you can't let them not play Saturday or Friday.

I did that a few times. I remember a parent calling me at home, angry because their son hadn't been at practice all week, so I said, you're not dressing for the game. So the parent called me at home, and he went through a whole list of things why what I did was wrong, and I said, "Well I feel pretty confident in the reasons why I made that decision." But it was all about his kid.

So why do you think, stepping back for a second, and we'll get to your dad in a little bit. Why do you think that's happening? Why do you think people have become that way? Do you think they don't get it, or why are parents doing that?

I don't know if they're living their life again through their kid and want to ease out all those bumps they might have experienced. I don't know.

So where did that become a right, that someone has their own cell phone and they don't pay for it?

I know, I lived through that beginning of the cell phone as an administrator. So our board had the initial policy of all cell phones should be turned off and out of sight. So then you dealt with kids in the classroom or the hallway and the teacher seeing it, teachers confiscating it, teachers bringing it down to the main office in an envelope with the kids name on it. Then you would have to deal with the kid or the angry parent. That consumed an unreal amount of time.

So why can't you just say, other then administration and teachers, cell-free zone? You bring a cell phone in this school, we're going to keep it, you're never getting it back. What stops people from doing that?

Well, an example I can think of is the new high school in London was built for Wi-Fi and built for like a paperless environment, and so they're encouraging kids to use their tablets, their laptops, cell phones.

So you think it's not just the kids, it's the whole culture that's changed?

Yes, you look at people and they can't survive without their phone, or if it beeps, they have to react to it right away, they've got to answer right away. Like if they get a text, it's not like it sits there until they're finished what they're doing if they're talking to somebody.

So did you ever hear the word "no" growing up?

Oh yeah.

Why do you think some kids have never heard that word?

Yeah, it's the whole philosophy I guess, if you want to be your kid's best friend opposed to their parent, right.

So let's go into you being a parent? You've got three girls. So how did you parent? What was your discipline to your children like?

When I was on my own, the youngest was seven, and the oldest was twelve. Middle one was ten. I wanted them to have stability, so I knew it was important.

John goes on to discuss his separation and not being officially separated until ten years later. So you would work, get home right away, and take care of the kids?

Well, they had basketball practice or whatever. My ex would help out, too, I have to give her credit for that.

She would pick them up at school or take them to the practice.

Okay, so I have to ask you because men will wonder. What stopped you from leaving? Because a lot of guys just leave.

Again, that whole thing about stability, and I think there is something in me to show people I can do it.

How tough was it?

I don't want to get emotional. (We take a break.)

I was going to talk to you about discipline with the girls.

Well, with the oldest, I think I spanked her once, and I felt so bad doing it that it never happened again. But not with the others.

Did you have grounding, or what did you do?

No, they were just very good kids.

So you kept the parental boundary?

Yeah, I wasn't their best friend. I was their dad. I would be the driver to drive them places, so I knew where they were going. They hung around with good kids, I knew the parents.

So tough question, but I want to ask you. How did you accept to yourself the sacrifices you made for your kids? Because you were a professional, and then you were a dad. You didn't have much time to do anything else for eighteen years.

Yes.

How did you, for eighteen years, give up yourself?

Well, I guess you're consumed with the things your kids are doing.

How do you handle losing? Do you think people need to win, or should everybody win?

No, I think you learn the most lessons when you lose.

I get the sense you weren't a good loser.

No, I don't think I still am. I'm stubborn that way.

Is there anything wrong with that?

Probably some people would tell me I'm stubborn, think there's something wrong with that.

Do you think it's observed, or learned or genetic? What's your gut tell you?

I think I take after my mother more than my dad, and she was very stubborn.

Did your daughters inherit that the stubbornness?

Yeah, I think one example is with my youngest, even when she was a little kid. What do you want to do when you grow up? I want to be a psychologist, a PhD, and you think okay, yeah sure right. Okay, we'll see if you get through high school first, and then university, but she stayed on that path, and at twenty-seven, she earned her PhD.

If we go back through everything you've told me about raising the girls, was what's best for them, not you. I mean it would have been easier for you to hand them off fifty percent of the time, but you made decisions for your kids that are best for them. When you tell them no, even though you can get them something. You say no, it kind of hurts because you want to give them something because it feels good to give stuff, especially if you didn't have it. But isn't that kind of the job?

Well, you're supposed to be their parent, not their friend. I think some people get caught up, that they don't want their kid to cry, or they don't want their kid to say I don't like you or whatever.

So what advice would you give if someone's having a child today, with regard to discipline?

I think you want to give them opportunities; you want them to experience a number of opportunities. See what they enjoy, make sure they have a strong home life.

What do you mean by strong home life?

Well, that there are loving parents there. There's a house

or a place they can call home, go home to every day. That they have stimulation of some nature, whether it's a toy or some game. They develop friendships and good quality friendships.

What about struggle? Do you think struggle is necessary?

Well, yeah, again losing is even more important than winning I guess. Not to make life easy. Don't bail them out, but be supportive of them. And an analogy that I can use maybe, and I don't know if this is really along that line, but in teaching, when you get the younger kids starting their teaching career, recently over the last ten years, those are all kids who were high academic achievers, never struggled in school. Easy, no problems or whatever, always the top-notch kid and then they'd be in their teaching career, they'd be teaching these kids that aren't motivated, and they had no idea on how to deal with them. I can remember, like those are the kids I liked to work with, because I knew what that was about. But that younger generation of teachers they have no idea.

Do you think you can change things as a teacher if the child comes without any discipline growing up?

All their life they've never had "no" at all. Everything Johnny does is amazing. I am sure it would take almost half the year to get them kind of in line with the structure. And they might then have a life at home where everything's good, and then the life at school they know there's structure. But you have to have structure in a classroom.

Is being too nice as a parent a form of abuse?

Yeah, I'm sure you're doing a big disservice to the child.

What do you think is important?

Again, I feel athletics gives you that structure, gives you that busyness to develop a schedule so you can get all those things done, and it's amazing how productive you can be when you're involved in sports. Plus, you develop friendships; you are associated with older people like your coaches that, hopefully, give you good lessons or good role models. It's the whole winning together, losing together, that experience is tremendous. You know you can't get that in the classroom.

No, maybe that's the answer, like with your kids and every-thing else, you just do it. You don't notice it. We are all around people who are called leaders, like actors, they didn't live it, they didn't feel it, they didn't demonstrate it.

Well yes, I think we've all seen that and experienced and you know whatever you call leadership or just getting the job done, you know, you got to do it. It's not a sprint; you got to do it day by day, one foot in front of the other. Get up the next morning, repeat the same process again or whatever.

But the point of all of that is quiet leadership?

I guess leadership is not necessarily in the eyes. Take me for example, it's not necessarily in me, believing I'm a leader or not believing I'm a leader, it's how other people perceive you. So if you're a leader, maybe it's because they perceive you as showing them the way or helping find their way, but you don't necessarily think of that, it's just what you do.

But isn't what you do like water, it's a fact, it's not a perception?

Well, yeah, what you do is what you think is right, what is just, what you have to do. Those people who are observing what you do and then they're calling that leadership. Maybe they're calling it leadership because they want to follow what you do.

Who was your mentor growing up?

I guess it would be my mom.

* * *

John "Lightning" Milne taught me many things over the years on the football field, and since then, about leadership. He developed his strong work ethic by watching his parents and hearing about his grandparents while he was only a child. Sports for him were the teacher of even more discipline outside of the home and his strong belief system, self-confidence in his ability to play football at a very high level.

He lead by example, then as a teacher, administrator, and father, he sacrificed his own personal wants and needs for the betterment of his children.

He heard the word "no" quite regularly, partly because his parents couldn't afford some things, and when they could, because they felt it wasn't necessary. He learned that you couldn't have everything you wanted as a child and that boundaries exist between parents and their children. Being a parent doesn't mean you are your child's friend.

I believe after studying the transcript of my interview with Lightning, that his character, strong work ethic, and leadership skills were well developed prior to his arriving at the University of Western Ontario. The parenting he received and the environment that he was in, combined with specific genetic characteristics, lead to his success as a leader on the football field, in schools, and as a father. There is much to learn from Lightning's examples of quiet leadership.

10

Natasha Borota

NATASHA BOROTA ESTABLISHED the It Factor in 2003, an events, marketing, and sports/celebrity management (Celebrity Shop) boutique agency. She is the co-founder and, until recently, the President of the Michael "Pinball" Clemons Foundation (MPCF). The foundation supports a number of charities to accomplish its "quest to make our community, country, and world a better place."

I initially reached out to Natasha through social media because of her involvement in the foundation and the example of philanthropy she has demonstrated throughout her life. I interviewed her at the It Factor offices in Toronto.

Born on January 2, 1971 she was the first natural-born child in Joseph Brant Hospital that year.

So when your mom was carrying you, what was life like for her?

You know what, I think it was fairly good. My father was a successful businessman in Canada, probably one of the company's top-five performers; he travelled a lot. I was not planned for, nor expected. I have a sister and brother who are one year apart, who were seven and eight years older than me…the white picket fence. I always say my claim to fame, and why God wanted me here, was my mother had an IUD, and I was born with it in my hand. So it was like an umbrella guiding me into the world.

Seriously?

Absolutely, I had it in my hand.

That's a great story. Do you have pictures?

I don't know if my mom has pictures, but the funny thing is she used to say, "I can't believe you tell people that story." And I'm like, "It's hilarious." The point is, I obviously wanted to be here.

So you're born. So your mom was good. Did your folks always live here?

No, I was born in Burlington, but they had lived in Edmonton and then London, Ontario, and so my sister and brother were born out of Burlington, but they had lived in Burlington for many years. My mom has a sad story. Her upbringing was challenged, to say the least, and she lived on her own since she was very young, first in a boarding house in Hamilton. Her family's from the States, but she was moved out West to work on a farm for her uncle as she had left a really bad situation and then moved into a rooming house in Hamilton. She went to night school to learn shorthand and became one of the VPs of Westinghouse's secretary by the age of sixteen or so. My father's family came from the old country, my daki "grandfather" owned land in Hamilton and emigrated from Serbia. They went to Hamilton, because there are many Serbian Orthodox families there. They owned a pool hall, and my father worked in the pool hall after school every day, and my mom and dad met at a community dance, I think, when they were around sixteen. So I always say my dad saved my mom, that God felt she needed to have a good life. She had been a really good girl and had serious struggles when she was younger, and my dad was her blessing from God. I think they got married in their early twenties, my sister was born and then my brother. My father travelled a lot with business. My mom could fortunately be a stay-at-home mom.

So compared to what she had before, it was great?

Yes, she was abused by her father and stepfather in different ways.

Did you ever meet the grandparents?

Yes, I met my grandfather, who was charged with

attempted murder on my mom's life. He came around when my grandmother passed, when I was young, and tried to insert himself into our family, and that wasn't going to happen. My mom didn't have a lot of her family to support her, but her challenges were mostly with my father's family, because my mom wasn't Serbian. Back in the day, you needed to marry a woman in your faith and religion, so there were challenges for them, and I would say there still are.

My mom handled it gracefully. She broke the chain of abuse. My mom never raised her hand or her voice. My father was definitely the disciplinarian. My mother I just have so much respect for her, and that is something where I got to always put things into perspective. She changed, you know most people, people let them off the hook by saying that, well, that's all they knew was abuse. So if your father was a cheater, your grandfather was probably a cheater, and they just, oh they learned a habit. And I one hundred percent believe that's a cop-out because I've seen my mother who could have, by all rights, continued that abusive behaviour on us, never one day. She honestly has the spirit of an angel.

Were you ever spanked?

Absolutely. I was the bad one out of all of them. I probably got it the most.

You had structure and discipline at home?

My father was the disciplinarian. I was probably the most challenging child for them because I was a little wilder than everybody. And I think most of my disciple came, I believe, not from me disrespecting them, but from me crossing boundaries. So coming in late, or being out with my friends, or being at the barn with my horse and not letting people know where I was and not having respect for the fact that that can cause a problem and make people worry. I wasn't a bad kid, as in drugs or alcohol or getting caught up in the "wrong" crowd. I probably was the crowd.

Were you always the person who would go left if others said to go right?

For sure, and most people followed me right. I've always been that leader, and that sort of got me in trouble, too, because I'd always push boundaries. Kids who might have been following me would get in trouble.

How did you get along with teachers?

Very well.

All of them?

No.

What about the ones you couldn't respect?

I think probably the ones who were weak. It is a great

trait to have, but I have always preyed on weak people, and I've also not been able to respect them.

Define prey.

You know I won't say take advantage in a negative way, but I knew what I could get away with. I was so strong. I'm very black and white. I don't worry about hurting people's feelings. I'd rather tell the truth. You're going to hurt them eventually, and it will be worse the longer you wait. I always say just rip off the Band-Aid.

What's your youngest nicest childhood memory?

This is a challenge for me, I don't remember a lot of my childhood. We would always travel to Florida for the winter, like for the holidays over the winter and my dad would drive. My father got to a point where he was terrified of planes because he had flown so much that he was like, "The law of averages, soon it's happening, and I don't want it to happen with my family."

Once something happened with our car when I was about ten, and we were on the side of the road because our car broke down. A trucker stopped and helped us, and I remember us getting his information and his address, and my mom and I went shopping as soon as we got to Florida and sent a huge Christmas package for his family. It showed me that my parents cared about human beings. So there was a lot of charity in my house. My parents supported the Salvation Army, more monetary, but they made sure we knew.

For you, it was the best memory because you saw your parents giving to someone else?

Yeah, it was like we could provide something for them, and because I couldn't, I was young, but I think I learned my first lesson about really helping somebody else when you can, and even if you can't, finding a way to do it.

What's your worst memory of childhood?

I was out late and I shouldn't have been, I was a figure skater and I rode horses and was always on the go. Probably thirteen, fourteen, and I was out with my girlfriend from down the street. She was a skater too. She was better than me because I really wanted to focus on horses more than anything. We stayed out late, just in our neighbourhood, but my dad went looking for me. I made it home before he got home and we lived in a small subdivision but there was a skating arena, a little corner store, like places to hang out if you are kids. And I had to sit out on the front lawn for the car to pull up, and I knew I was getting it. I knew I was getting it.

Did he spank you?

Yeah, probably that night.

How many times do you think you were spanked in your life?

Minimal. It was always for something big. Five to eight times in all probably. Otherwise it would be maybe a swat.

What did you watch your parents do as far as work goes? Was dad a hard worker?

Oh, absolutely. My dad's work ethic was great. He was always on the road, he was always working. My mom started small businesses when we got older. She and my sister opened a store in Burlington; it was a high-end furniture and interior store. So before all these big box stores came, she was the place to go if someone wanted unique items.

In Burlington, on her own?

Yup, with my sister. It was on Fairview Street. So she started that business and they stayed in business for about twenty years, and then my dad retired. They are each other's best friend; they don't have a lot of friends outside of each other. I used to think how romantic, because when my father was with this larger company, they would have a lot of parties, there would be a lot of temptation for the successful business guys, and you know, sometimes even the women if the men are gone. And I think they always felt like, in order to keep their marriage and our family strong, it was important that they didn't associate a lot outside of work, in those situations.

Work was work. Now that my father's ill and my mom has found other ways, like I took my mom to my church.

My mom was always a believer, but when she was a kid growing up, she wasn't able to go to church due to the situation of how she grew up, but she always had a relationship with God, but she wasn't very versed in the Bible and in the word of God and understanding that there's proof behind everything that he says he can do as our Saviour.

As I got older and I started searching, and I was more involved in the church, my mom went to my Bible study teacher whose husband is the chaplain for the CFL and the Raptors. But his wife was one my Bible study teachers when I came back from university, twenty-something years ago. So I connected them, and she took my mom through the program. My mom actually now does a small women's Bible study on Wednesdays, and it gave her an outlet to focus on and women to learn from and be associated in that positive area.

But I am going say that I remember when my dad worked for a large company and then he went out on his own, and basically, even after he retired, he always kept his foot in the door of smaller projects and contracting to people that were in small business to help them develop their business plans and things like that. I did notice that once it got to be where you couldn't do business on a handshake anymore and things got very cutthroat that he backed away.

Are you a person who can do business by handshake?

I am, but I have been burnt when I haven't put the paperwork in order because that person hasn't followed through with what their handshake was committed to. So absolutely, if I tell you I'm doing something, I'm doing it, right at the end of the day. Just you stick to your word. You give a hundred and ten percent. You under-promise and over-deliver.

Did you hear yes for everything you asked for as a kid?

Absolutely not.

That was quick.

No, no. They could have said yes, they were in position to say yes, but they wanted us to learn what it was to work for things.

Do you think that was hard for them to say?

I think it was harder for my mom because of her background. I think because she always wanted to be better than what she had had. I think for my father, he knew what it took, how hard he worked to get what he had, so it was almost a pleasure to give us things that he couldn't have growing up. They had left family members behind and had to come here to sponsor them to bring everybody over from Serbia. So my father would go in at five thirty in the morning to clean the pool hall from the night before, because he would have to close it at one in the morning. Right, well you can't stay and clean it up too when you have to go to school. And he never said when I was there, we had to walk ten miles to go to school.

The stories came from my Bubbi I think and watching how hard they worked. So at eighty years old, they were still active and going to the market every weekend and taking public transit around the east end of Hamilton. So I guess you get a different upbringing when your family has had to come from the old country, where you lived off the farm. Where you woke up every day and did chores before you went to school. You came home, you worked 'till sundown. I feel like it's the best thing they could have done.

I was into horses at a really young age, but I had to work at the barn that I was leasing a horse from to pay the lease for my horse or the board. I had to muck every stall that was on my list, clean water buckets.

How old were you?

From ten to fifteen. Then I started to realize I wanted to do this for a career and it became more important to me, and when I was going away to university to the States, Louisiana Tech University, my whole education is in horses. I was a thoroughbred racehorse trainer.

You wanted to be a vet?

No, I didn't want to be a vet, but I had to get a bachelor of animal science which is your pre-vet because my parents wouldn't let me continue on to do something like that without degrees. So they understood I wanted to do something with horses, they also understood you better find something that can pay your bills.

Why did you pick that university?

I went to the top three in the nation for a thoroughbred racehorse training program, and when we visited all the schools, the doctor who was running that school is actually the real horse whisperer.

So you go to high school, how was high school?

High school was good. I went to, like, a prioritized learning school for my last year.

What's that?

I don't know, they say gifted or challenged in traditional learning intuitions.

Well, you don't believe that, that you're gifted?

No, I think I'm gifted in other areas. I'm a doer, so sitting down and doing something I didn't feel was going to be able to help me in the future was hard for me to understand. I wanted to get out, get to the barn. I always had good grades; I wrote my SATs and went to school in the States.

You finished school in the States, and then what do you do?

I actually already had my trainer's license. I was the youngest female to get a trainer's license in the State of

Louisiana. So I got my thoroughbred racehorse trainer's license while I was in university. Bought a yearling, therefore, I was at the barn every morning at six a.m. long before classed started.

You bought some horses in university?

Yup, some cheap Louisiana breed, but you know the board for them was paid for because I worked at the training barn at school, and then I broke them and tried to get them to the races with other horses in our barn. They were our projects.

How did they do?

One made it to the races, the other one was injured. She never broke her maiden, but she ran like a second or third, but we paid a thousand dollars for her, if I recall. It was the experience of having, number one, to get my education, so get to class; do my work; get my grades, but also the responsibility of being at the barn seven days a week, three hundred sixty-five days a year, working. There's a big difference when you work in agriculture or in this type of business I do now.

The unfortunate thing is, I have a hard time managing my time now. I continuously work because it's just bred into me. So when I came out of school, I became an assistant trainer to a successful trainer at the track, I gave up my trainer's license to work for him and get some experience, because you have to find owners to hire you to train as a public trainer. I was not independently wealthy, and I'm an educated female coming into a male dominated business, which already was two strikes against me, I had to make it on my own.

I came to Woodbine; I had worked there in the summers. I picked different trainers every summer to work for during university, so I could see how they trained. I was in their back pockets, paying attention to what was going on. I was a groom, so I would take care of my four or five horses a day, so I learned a lot. I worked for claiming trainers; I worked for trainers that only had stake horses, a broad spectrum.

When I came back, I became an assistant for a success-ful claiming trainer who always had a good horse or two mixed in, but he had like thirty-six head of horses at all times, always running. So I thought the best thing for me to do is to work for a big shed, be an assistant, so you do all the work because the trainer at that point, you know, most cases doesn't do much if they're not hands-on. They rely a lot on their assistants. So all the medications, watching the horses train, setting up what exercise rider is galloping who, working with vets on injuries…basi-cally assisting with everything.

I did that for a couple of years. I was only going to do it for one year and then go out on my own, but we had a really nice horse and her leg was put on backward. She had a serious knee problem, due to a foot issue. But probably one of the best horses I've ever had my hands on as a racehorse, I stayed there for her whole three-year-old campaign and most of her four-year-old campaign.

Do you think will is more important than talent? Have the will to win?

I think everybody has talent. What makes you a champion is the will, the drive and your work ethic. It comes down to *heart*!

Big heart, bad leg.

Yeah, so I wanted to stay with her for another year because we had a campaign for her going down to the States to run in a couple of really great stake races, and I felt like without me he was a claiming trainer. So he trained horses hard, into the ground. That's his style, which is fine, it was his style. You claim a horse, they might be in your barn for two races, you get the most out of them, you try to sell them for a higher level of claiming when you get them to win, and then the next one comes in. So when you have these other horses, it's a lot about nurturing them and making sure you pay attention to everything that happens to them.

You know what they like, you pay attention to their moods, you know when they don't feel well, and you know when you should back off, when you should go a little further, so I felt like I should stay with her. I stayed an extra year with them and we had an amazing campaign with her, and then I went and claimed a couple of horses on my own, and then I got a couple of private owners that gave me their horses, so I had a racing stable, which was really nice for me and the majority were fairly good horses. I didn't have a lot of claimers. I had some gentlemen who bred their own horses.

Actually, they were both in the food industry. I had a little horse that I claimed for sixteen thousand dollars, a Texas bred that just made me who I was. I claimed him for sixteen, and he went through all of his allowances two-fifths off the track record twice, and I still have him. He's retired in a little Christian hockey and horse riding camp.

Doesn't he get the urge to take off once in a while?

He did for a while. The kids would never ride him; he's only for the people that work there to ride, but he was so miserable retired in a field, and I didn't have a lot of time to ride him, he simply liked to work. He was a kind horse; he had a quarter horse's behaviour, which is so much calmer than the usual thoroughbred's high-strung character.

His demeanour was kind, whereas thoroughbreds, when they're ready to run, they're aggressive, they'll hurt you. A lot of times they're not hurting you on purpose, it's the hormones, and you think about it. One of my client's last night, a top receiver in the NFL, made an amazing block, he blocked for another receiver to get a touchdown, and at the end of that, you could see he felt just as full of himself for making that block as the receiver that got credited for the score. The power and strength

142

you saw in him after, it's almost like it's an uncontrollable thing, your adrenaline takes over.

So horses don't necessarily mean to hurt humans, a lot of it is we've got them wound up like alarm clocks, just waiting to go off, to get them to the races on their game. So the funny thing is, that's sort of what I've taken from my old business into the new one, almost having an understanding of what pro athletes have to do to succeed.

Why did you stop doing it?

Oh, I hurt my back about thirteen years ago really bad. I was at a point where I had two herniated disks, and I have a piece of my vertebra sitting on my spinal column. I had a couple of accidents; a horse threw me into a wall. A couple of things happened over time, and I've gotten degenerative joint disease in my back.

You're going to have to retire like an athlete?

Pretty much.

How did that go?

Not so well, I mean it was a challenge. It's my passion; it's the only thing I've wanted to do in my life. I was born to be with horses.

How do you get from that to this?

I mean I had built a pretty good database. Going to university, a lot of guys I knew went and played pro sports, and I had always kept in touch with all these guys. I had a couple of little guys who were interested in racing, so I might have had an inclination on a horse or two. So they would come out to the races, and next thing you know, I've got a guy from the Jets at my race, the next thing you know, he brings his buddy who plays for the Knicks.

So you're building this database, and for some reason, it was heavy with celebrity and big shooters. I was fairly well-known and people recognized me a lot when I was a trainer, but it was a very cutthroat business, it's a hard business, and I retired basically.

How old were you when you retired?

I'm going to say thirty-one, thirty-two.

You had to sell your horses?

Yeah well, I didn't own a lot of them. I had to get other people to train; they had to find other trainers at the track. It got to be every morning I'd be crying, trying to put my socks on, right, and I never woke up a day in my life until then, not a day, saying I didn't want to go to work at five a.m. Didn't matter if I went to bed at two, I was excited to go see the horses. I'm being honest, I never ever one day didn't want to get up and go to work.

How long was the transition from horses to this?

It sort of happened right away, I didn't really take any

time off. What I did was I had always been connecting different athletes to different organizations, so I was philanthropic in a way and never knew it; I also attended a lot of charity events. I started realizing how these athletes and their celebrity really helped to promote different organizations and get exposure for them, and then people would ask me, well, would he come out to our golf tournament and speak, maybe play golf.

I would start to get guys paid for that, but I never took any money from it because I was still training. I just thought… hey, one day I'll be doing something and I'll ask for a favour, and there you go. So that's sort of how it started, and then I was at an event, and I always say this, Pinball said to me, I had booked him a few times, and he and his wife were becoming good friends of mine, and he didn't really know what I was challenged with at the time, and one day we were talking, and I said, "You know this is sort of my challenge." And he said, "Well, you're fire, like what you do connecting people, I'll work with you."

Pinball said he would work with you?

Yes, and he does to this day.

We all know him in Canada.

I mean he's well known in the States too, but outside of sports, he's well-known for the causes he supports. Not just philanthropic, but in business as the chairman as the Argos now. So he said, you know I'll work with you a hundred percent. You're good at this. I still didn't know what I was going to do, and like I said, I was challenged in deciding what I do. I was an accredited steward, so I could have just stayed at the racetrack in a different facet of the business; a steward, they basically enforce the laws of the racetrack.

Referee of horses?

Yeah, and they watch the races, so if a jockey calls an inquiry, they would do that too. So if somebody's brought up on drug charges for their horse, that would go to the steward and they would have to go through their book of laws and rules and regulations and be able to rule.

Like a horse cop?

Absolutely, but without being a cop. Like on a different level, more of a business level.

You could have done that?

Absolutely. I had gone and gotten my accreditation at the University of Kentucky.

That was your second degree, that's right.

I'm a certified sports massage therapist for equine, all my education's in horses. So it just so happens that I better figure something out, because now I got to pay the bills, and then I bumped into a world champion boxer who came up and did an event because Mohammed Ali was participating with the Argos, and I asked Mike if he wanted him to attend as well. Absolutely, he said, who wouldn't want him. His first time in Canada, and he came up to support me at this event that just fit...things were just moving into place for my next career.

The Raptors happened to be playing, and I got us seats and we sat courtside. So there's a lady I'm always looking at, and I'd always say to Mike, one day we're going to be working with her, I just know. I saw her and her husband and they'd always be courtside, and they were movers and shakers.

And then I found out that she was on the board of a big children's hospital here in the city. He said why don't you just go and introduce yourself. Funny thing is, she was telling her husband the same thing about me. I don't know who that girl is, but I need to meet her and find out how she knows all these people. And he said to her, why don't you introduce yourself? So one day she introduced herself to me. They had a friend who had a marketing business, and they thought we should meet.

I'm like, I'm trying to find my way now, I'm between things, sort of, God's shut this door, which I thought would never be shut in my lifetime. It's what I've always wanted to do, and I've got to jump though whatever door he opens for me. I have a database of all these guys, I can make them money off the court, off the field, off the ice. I have the ability to use their name and likeness; I just need to figure out how to do that. My education is in horses, but I can sell myself, which is the key.

So he introduced me to his best friend at the time at that company, and I said, "Hey, you have all the contacts to all the marketing agencies, I have the contacts to celebrities. Let's come up with contests, sweepstakes, and promotions to utilize them, get my guys paid, get me paid, and you're a hero because you're now able to bring all these guys in." So then he and I, within a week, partnered together, and we never signed a contract in almost a decade just worked off a handshake.

It worked?

It worked, yup, we never agreed to anything, either way. So it ended up that there was an organization that I was already working with celebrities that had an RFP out to run a huge event. A fundraiser that they had run internally, and they wanted to take it external and try to make it bigger and get exposure and somehow we got on the RFP thing. I had already had an association to them; he nor I, had ever run an event. We said, well let's just try, so we are completely the dark horse, like we're going up against event companies with twenty-five years' experience, but we won the RFP. So now we have to figure out how to do execute.

You agreed to do everything, even though you didn't know?

Oh absolutely, we got it and it was successful, and we

actually had the contract for seven years. So he and I parted ways. I had started the IT Factor at that time, and he had another business. So we chose to grow that business because the IT Factor was more just the sport celebrity marketing division, like more of my celebrity show. I had never thought about doing events; I had thought about marketing my guys, right.

Doing a sports agency?

A hundred percent, and I actually was the youngest female licensed sports agent in Canada.

Still do that big time?

Don't do any contracts; not interested. I only do personal service agreements, speaking engagements, run their charity events.

Outside sports for them. Or in sports, but it's not about their contact with the team, it's about all the other stuff?

That's right. So I would go to the team to get sponsorship for something I'm doing for them for a charity event, but their contact is with their agent, and I do things outside of that. Their car deals, their personal appearances, personal service agreements. We're a small boutique agency.

So the other part is the philanthropic work you do, the giving and the charity. Where does that come from, from how you were parented? You talked about your mom taking in your friends and stuff. Where do you think that came from? That you're so focused on also helping?

I think it's my mom. She has a kind heart. And I help more than I should. It has been a detriment to my business as far as getting the numbers up.

But isn't this who you are as a person?

That's right. But I need to find a better balance, and I think I'm doing it now. A lot of things I did were sweat equity. I'm running the business, but I'm also giving hours and hours and hours of my time, unpaid. Hence hours away from mentoring the ladies that are working with me at my small business. Hours away of not making them number one because my foundation needed me. I didn't have any staff for five years. So I am running my small business and running the foundation.

The foundation is pro bono?

I had no staff. I never took a dollar.

What's the focus of the foundation?

I managed everything, so I did all the paperwork; I did everything at the foundation. Got it started, and we are very youth motivated. So character building, education, trying to create better citizens, and health for under-resourced kids. So our mandate was fifty percent to stay in

Southern Ontario, or in our community, fifty percent in under-resourced countries.

We're finishing our third campaign, which would put us at two hundred and sixty-two schools and seven under-resourced countries. This is our ninth year, and now there's a paid staff, I had to separate myself to focus on the business because the staff need to do their job. It was very hard because it was like giving birth to something, like that's my baby, that's my child, but my business was definitely being challenged for the fact that I was spread too thin.

Do you consider yourself a leader?

Absolutely, yeah.

Do you think you do it, or do you consciously think about leading people?

No, I think I need to consciously think about it more. But I just do it.

Where do you think that comes from? The leadership piece.

I think the leadership piece comes from my dad. My dad was strong, dominate, and I got his personality. I guess the other thing was going away to university, to the South. Going to university in the South, being challenged by having the morals and integrity and was brought to me here of everybody being the same. My parents coming from the old country, like I'm not Canadian. I'm now Canadian by choice, however I'm Serbian. That's my background, that's where my father is from.

We have such a multicultural country here, that it was a challenge being there. I always try to break those barriers that were happening. So I spent a lot of time at Grambling, I took classes at Grambling State, which is a black college three miles down the road. Most of my minor came from there because of the fact that I felt much more comfortable at Grambling being the minority, then I did at Tech and seeing what was instilled in most of the people that were there from the South. And I say most, as in most. There were people who were more open-minded, but it definitely was two separate sides of the track.

Are your parents proud of you? Do you hear that from them?

Not in those words, but they like to hear about what I'm doing, and they are supportive and always want to hear about our successes or challenges at the office. So I would say that my dad wasn't a real emotional guy, like, we weren't hugging all the time. But I one hundred percent knew that he was proud of me. I think one of the biggest compliments he can give me today is the fact that in the hospital, he is relying on me to be able to hear him and know that I'm strong enough to handle his burden right now.

What's the role of faith in your life?

God's my Saviour, and I believe that nothing happens without him walking hand in hand with me.

Did that come from your parents?

Mom had a great relationship with God, a personal relationship with God, but we didn't go to church a lot. We were that Orthodox family: Easter, Christmas, somebody dies, sitting, listening to my Orthodox bishop speaking in old Serbian. But I always knew that something guided my mom. Like the light in her was from somewhere, so I was always searching for that.

She'd always speak to me about Jesus, and when I went away to school and I was so challenged with trying to figure out how do I live in this society because this isn't me. And how do I live here and get my education without blackballing myself from everything at the same time. I definitely got saved in college. I slept a few nights in a little church that I found open at two a.m. one night when I was out and was dealing with something. Slept there that night, obviously, and asking God to give me the strength to continue what I was doing and be who I was and not to succumb to other people's values and what I know is not right.

From that day in university, I have continuously strived to create a better relationship with God. Rely on him more, and less on myself, and understand that without him, none of what I have is possible and to be grateful every day for what I have and try and keep things in perspective and know I don't have control. I can be the best person I can be, I can work as hard as I can to help other people, and that's what I'm here for: to let people know

153

that by the grace of God, I have what I have. And it might look more glamorous to them because people see what I do for a living and they think it's so glamorous, but it is really hard work. I'm also so aware that without him in my life, I wouldn't be where I am.

Five years from now where are you going to be? What are you going to be doing?

I hope to have my business up and running in Arizona. I'm really proud of my NFL clients and my relationship with them. Mike's an unbelievable human being, but I think my gift is helping these athletes or celebrities to reach their goals and create their future outside of their present jobs. They're so humble, but helping them recognize how much their celebrity can affect change if they use it and what they can achieve in a completely different industry, recognizing their future, and attaining other goals and dreams, is an awesome space to be in.

Final thoughts?

I wish other kids had parents like mine, that pushed me to be better. That wanted me to be a good citizen, and they taught me right from wrong. It was hard to understand why and was challenging at times, but they also ruled with a semi-iron fist, for which I am grateful.

* * *

Driving away from the interview, I was moved at Natasha's dedication to helping others, and her strong faith in God that continues to drive her purpose and work. Oppositional but tempered, an example to both men and women seeking to learn what childhood experiences can lead to greatness. Her parents must be so very proud.

11

Parenting and Blueberry Pie

I LOVE BLUEBERRY pie, especially those made from the small blueberries found in Northern Ontario. If you close your eyes for a minute, I want you to imagine a pie is cooling on top of a stove with the smell of fresh baking filling the room.

The pie as it sits, represents the sum total of the factors that contribute to your child becoming a strong leader. If you think of those factors as each piece of the six-piece blueberry pie, I believe that the factors that influenced the creation of our leaders to be:

1. Genetics

2. Environment

3. Random Chance

4. Parenting – Unconditional Love and Observational Learning

5. Parenting – Hearing the word "No" regularly and Discipline

6. Parenting – Oppositional Behaviour and Winning

A child may become a strong leader despite all of the mistakes you make, or the fact you aren't engaging in any of the strategies you are about to learn. You may get lucky. Genetics and environment may override the lack of courage you display when raising your child. As well, you can do everything you possibly can as a parent, do all of the right things, and still have a child that struggles and is unable to take on the world and lead with confidence. Genetics, environment, and random chance may be responsible for this.

But don't you want to give your child, grandchild, nephew, or niece the best possible opportunity to become a strong leader?

My message to you is it is your *obligation*. It's not your choice.

Before I get into the six strategies you need to use, let me explain the goals of your child and the parenting task as we take your child from conception to adulthood at the age of forty.

12

Stages of Child and Parental Development Today

UNTIL NOW, CHILD development has focused on developmental periods that generally talk about reaching adulthood at age sixteen or eighteen. But today, eighteen is more like the new twelve, twenty-one the new fourteen, and so on. Children take longer to develop because they are exposed to many more things that weren't available when you were growing up. The extended childhood trend is also linked to what we now know about our neurological or brain development. Children, teenagers, young adults, and even seniors develop cognitively until their death. There does not now seem to be a period of time when we stop developing or learning. Parenting strategies need to adapt to this new reality.

In reading about the six leaders in this book, you likely

noticed how they have somewhat similar stories. Often during my interviews with them, they were surprised by the similarity in their giving or sharing with others' behaviour that was identical to that of their parents. They were just "doing it" without thought of any personal gain or reward or intentional action. In most cases, they were around, sometimes watching their parents, other times not. I call the influence of the parents that happen without direct intention, just by being around them, the Sponge Factor.

The **SPONGE FACTOR** is the power of your child, soaking into their brain, all that is around them with regard to observational learning. I believe at some level, at early ages, these observations, senses of fear and danger, discipline, sharing, caring, empathy, all they watch you do, become "hardwired" into their brain. Of course, this is an observational fact, if you will, that I present to you here in this book. Neuroscientists are able to identify "trauma" parts of our brain and "pain" for example, but little research has been done to find out the "giving," "empathy," "kindness," or "leadership" parts. I believe soon we will know this.

For the stages below, I have adjusted the size of the Sponge Factor text to reflect what I feel is the power of this on your child at each developmental stage. The Sponge Factor is something I learned in listening to the six stories of the leaders in this book. It is important for you to remember this when you are looking at your own actions around your child. It is also of utmost importance for aunts, uncles, grandmothers, and grandfathers. All play a part in influencing child cognitive and leadership development.

CONCEPTION TO TWO YEARS OF
AGE SPONGE FACTOR

Parent Goal: Provide physical and psychological safety-biological-psychological needs met. Reduce stress for mom to moderate at best while carrying the baby. Some minor stresses and struggles for mom may be positive from conception to birth. This is worthy of further study. The moms of most of the leaders in this book experienced some form of stress while carrying their child.

Child Goal: Birth-Survival. There are also psychological goals of bonding to significant others, and depending on the child's cognitive development, moving into areas of symbolic representation of feelings, thoughts, and emotions.

AGE THREE–SEVEN SPONGE FACTOR

Parent Goal: Establish routine, safe place for the child to return to when in time of stress, failure or need for positive encouragement to seek out independence. Discipline in terms of expectations, structures, rules, and routines. Saying "no" is a common parental response to most requests. Creation of work situations of a limited nature for the child is a mandatory goal.

Child Goal: Become physically able to leave situations, leave the crib, then room, then backyard, then to school. Be able to psychologically manage being away from family within a school environment. Learn to accept differences.

AGE EIGHT–THIRTEEN SPONGE FACTOR

Parent Goal: continue to support the child in moving away with continued ability of the child to see the parents as a safe haven for advice and encouragement. Parents provide continued significant structure and discipline based on the child's age and developmental level. Part-time work, involvement in sports, or the arts is required. Home duties for pay and for no pay as well as money management is introduced and encouraged with real-life application. "If you can't afford it, you can't have it" replaces "no."

Child Goal: Get away from parents, more freedoms and ability to control the world. Seeking of structure from the parents, but on the other hand, fighting to comply with it. Without structure and discipline, it breaks down very quickly. Psychosexual development becomes prominent goal.

AGE FOURTEEN–EIGHTEEN SPONGE FACTOR

Parent Goal: Structure and discipline peak at the age of fifteen–sixteen, with gradual reduction in this structure to prepare for expulsion from the nest. The final year of high school, the child has fewer rules than ever, parents watching closely to see how this freedom is handled. Again, parents are there to be the safe haven for discussion and support.

Child Goal: Prepare to leave home with continual forays into longer stays away. Learning to manage freedoms such as driving, voting, and, in some cases, legal alcohol consumption become primary challenges.

AGE NINETEEN–TWENTY-FIVE SPONGE FACTOR

Parent Goal: Support the child with psychological support for independence. Rewarding of such independence, and continue to move into a more mentor role. Confidence that your child can manage day-to-day living away from the home builds child self-esteem. Clear boundaries established between child and parent—adjusted to new age realities.

Child Goal: Ongoing continued move to independence with regard to relationships, financial growth, and career development. First job or post-secondary education now complete, decisions are needed on future goals to include graduate school or other academic degrees. Starting a small business is becoming more of an option for young adults today.

AGE TWENTY-SIX–FORTY SPONGE FACTOR

Parent Goal: Parent Mentor. Support of money management and career for the child. If need be, trials of "gifting" to view and advise the child on how to manage and invest those funds that may be inherited. Parent is primarily an observer of child reactions to these gifts.

Child Goal: Begin to develop permanence in relationships and career. Initiating of family life, partners, and connections to the community become more possible with identity formation.

AGE FORTY AND BEYOND SPONGE FACTOR

Parent Goal: Ongoing mentorship with the joy of sharing success—this is where you are rewarded for all of that hard work as a parent. This may happen in the previous stage if the parent is lucky. Starting over, helping in the parenting of grandchildren, and continuing to reward and comment on success and confidence that your child is capable of taking on the world without you.

Child goal: Build career, family, and personal life. Access to parent as mentor and occasional helper.

* * *

While all years are important, not surprisingly, the early years of a child's life when they are most vulnerable are the times when the Sponge Factor has the most power. It does not diminish, however, the importance you play in the life of your child after the age of twenty-five. Now after all of this, let me give you the six strategies to help you Parent with Courage and raise a Strong Leader.

13

The Six Strategies to Parent with Courage, But Wait a Minute, this isn't Rocket Science.

IT'S NOT COMPLICATED.

In fact, if you review my list below with a grandparent, or someone over the age of seventy-five, they likely will nod and tell you they knew this all along and didn't need a psychologist or a book to tell them what your job as a parent was. The challenge, of course, is to use the strategies within today's context of technology and rapidly evolving family structures to apply these strategies.

Here are my six strategies for you to start using today, so that you can Parent with Courage.

1. Building Unconditional Love

Unconditional love is defined as demonstrated love to

your child, regardless of their behaviour. You love them regardless of what they may say or do. That doesn't mean you tolerate it or don't provide that love within a disciplined environment. All six of the leaders interviewed had access to this on a regular basis from parents or grandparents who parented them. Here is the exercise that works for all ages that you can start using today.

Set aside thirty minutes on a calendar when you and your child will be alone. No distractions, no television, no video games (although for children eighteen or older, video games are fine), but an activity that your child chooses that, ideally, will only be used during that thirty minutes. It could be craft supplies, a special Lego set, anything within reason and for little cost, that your child chooses.

When the date and time comes each week, sit with your child, bring out the activity materials, and simply ask them, "What would you like me to do?"

Often your child will simply say, "Watch me." In my office when in the sandbox with children while parents observe, this is the most often request of a child.

The only rule is no aggression or destruction of property. The activity should not be competitive. When the thirty minutes are up, put the objects away and then schedule the next session for the following week. If you have more than one child, you need thirty minutes for each child, each week. For two parent families each parent needs to do the thirty minutes separately each week, for each child.

Each time you complete a thirty-minute play session you are building your child's self-esteem and their solid, secure rock from which they will take on the world. It also provides a base for you from which to deliver the discipline you will need to provide the proper structure for your child.

Discipline without unconditional love is destructive and rarely helpful in the parenting process.

I have previously discussed a strategy that I learned at Michigan State University in the 1980s as originally pioneered by Dr. Bernard Guerney. Filial therapy is the teaching of parents to be "therapists" to their children. It is the purest form, in my opinion, of building unconditional love experiences with your child.

The six strong leaders in this book all discussed such experiences with their parents that happened randomly and by chance. There were no Guerney Fillial parenting sessions for them, but rather times in the car driving to sporting events, time working as a carpenter's assistant, times where the child felt they were all that mattered to their parent at that time or moment. Today, we need to structure those times because, unless we do, they won't happen. Cell phones and instant access to work prevents the consistent random delivery of unconditional love experiences by parents to their children. You need to do this exercise, setting deliberate scheduled times, or it won't happen.

Remember, engaging in this activity does not mean you sit at the computer while your child plays on the floor with toys. All electronics, cell phones, and phones are disabled. Nothing is more important than the thirty minutes you are spending with your child at the time.

2. You demonstrate positive examples to enhance the Sponge Factor, including work ethic.

What your child is able to see, hear, or feel becomes a strong influence on your child developing strong leadership skills.

A second common trait to model, viewed by our leaders was the practice of pushing away emotions and pain—toughness—that's they watched their parents display. You need to understand the power of the sponge factor, that everything you do is part of what your child has learned. Being mentally tough and focusing on those things you can control sends the message to your child that living life as a victim isn't an option. Regardless of what happens, you control what you do with that event or situation. Being tough at a time of crisis by taking action is the example you want to set for your child.

3. Hearing the word "No" on a regular basis.

There are two types of no that were reported by our leaders.

Natural "No" refers to those situations that a parent is unable to fulfill, because they do not have the funds or resources.

Strategic "No" because the parents knew that giving them everything they wanted was a mistake, so even though they could afford it, parents of our Leaders said No to requests on a regular basis.

Regardless if Natural or Strategic, children, teens, and young adults need to hear this magic word to encourage, growth, development, desire for achievement, and appreciation for success. The frequency would change over the developmental time period, where a three-year-old may hear "no" many times over the course of one day, a sixteen-year-old may hear it once or twice a week. No rule on this one, just get used to it becoming part of your regular response to your child. All of our leaders interviewed for this book heard the word "no" on a regular basis.

4. **Discipline—age appropriate that for all of the six leaders in this book also represented corporal punishment or spanking or some other exposure to strong discipline.**

While not the primary method of discipline for any of the leaders in this book, spanking seems to send the message that parents are in control and rules must be followed.

Establishing logical consequences for behaviour, which are similar to what is provided if one were to make a mistake as an adult, is the goal. If you break a window as a forty or ten-year-old, the consequence is pretty much the same. You have to pay for the damage, apologize, and then take steps to reduce the chances of it ever happening again.

The tone of discipline is also about expectations.

If you take a farm example, at six in the morning, seven days a week, the animals must be fed, cleaned, and taken care of. The structure of discipline would be that the eight-year-old would get up and help the family take care of those duties. This is a type of discipline that then is transferred to the child and becomes an expectation that goes beyond the farm example. The child who gets up to help the family on the farm, most teachers would say, is a joy to work with because of the character built by that discipline.

Unfortunately, today, you likely don't live on a farm and don't have to get up to feed the animals. You may have a pet that needs walking, breakfast that needs to be prepared, lunches to be made, and so on. An elderly neighbour may need help shoveling snow, or getting breakfast or perhaps having the grass cut. Whatever you can create to enhance the environment of discipline and the expectation of contribution to others without gain for oneself, is part of the discipline process.

Being in charge of your home, or the boss, is your job as a parent. Your child will never have equal status in your home, because it is yours. They will move on and be motivated to establish their own rules and lifestyle in their own homes because that is the only way it is going to happen. In your home, you set the rules and the expectations. That will never change even when you are eighty-five and your child is fifty years of age.

5. **All of our six leaders witnessed in their parents, and were exhibiting themselves, different forms of Oppositional Defiance, fighting to be right and fighting to go against what others were telling.**

For some of our leaders this was obvious outside of the parenting situation, where in sports they didn't listen when others told them they were too small, too short, not fast enough, or the wrong gender to take on a career or profession. Being oppositional can be a very challenging trait to parent and manage, but once the oppositional child is contained by your ability to parent with courage, a key component of strong leadership will emerge.

6. **Only being the best matters. Winning is very important. It's expected. All of our six leaders hate to lose. This fight to win will propel your child to become a strong leader.**

Today, we often witness situations in sport or early life, where children are encouraged to participate where winning doesn't matter—ever. This is a colossal mistake that is all too common today. There are times when the stage is set to participate in an activity for no other purpose other than to enjoy that activity. If you take up fly-fishing for example, the purpose is to participate and, for myself, stand in a stream, enjoying the outdoors regardless if I win a fish or two or not (that I then release anyway). I've set the stage for fly-fishing to be participation, not a winning sport.

You need to teach your child, however, that in some activities, winning is the most important thing. All of our six leaders have this trait. When they are in their element, their sport, profession, or other activity they choose, winning, and being the best, is the focal goal.

As a parent, you need to give your child the opportunity to win and lose. It is the exposure to these opportunities that is your job. You can't control the outcome, but you need to expose your child to the realities that as an adult there will be times when you win, and many more when you lose. You need to practice and rehearse how to do that, at a very early age.

In summary, to Parent with Courage you need to build unconditional love, lead by example to enhance the Sponge Factor, say the word "no" on a regular basis, create an environment of discipline, embrace but temper oppositional behaviour, and create opportunities for winning and losing.

14

Your Action Plan

HERE ARE THE steps I'm recommending you start with right now to learn to Parent with Courage.

1. Share the ideas and concepts in this book with all of the mentors that will have influence on your child. Grandparents, aunts, uncles need to be on the same page with the six strategies as outlined.

2. If you didn't experience unconditional love as a child, you can learn how to experience this as an adult and then use the strategy with your children. Define unconditional love to those around you, your spouse, your own adult parents if possible. Acceptance and love based on you, not on your accomplishments, status, or achievements. Take thirty minute, weekly times to work on your own unconditional love exercise. It will make

a difference. Start with the calendar today and make sure you schedule your quality time, thirty minutes a week with your child. Take a trip with them to buy crayons, pencils, or paper or other supplies, specifically for the next time you engage in that activity.

3. Write down the key indicators of what you feel represents strong leadership and integrity. Where do you excel and what areas do you need to work on? Leading by example means that, firstly, you understand what you are communicating then you can make those improvements to lead by example and maximize the sponge factor for your child.

4. Practice saying the word "no" on a regular basis. You need to say this in your adult life so it becomes much easier to say to your child. Be honest and only use the Natural No if it is true. Strategic No only requires the following: "The answer is no because I said so, and I am in charge of that decision." Remember in your home, just like in life, often a "no" from someone doesn't allow for a negotiation.

5. Create rules and structure of discipline in your home, and make sure that everyone that is assisting your child agrees with their implementation. This can be such a challenge that I've created an online class for you to take at my practice site www.drsvec.com. I provide you a series of five minute or less modules to give

174

you examples and help you build the courage to discipline your child.

6. Embrace oppositional behaviour in a way to encourage it, but not to offend. In the online class mentioned above, I provide a specific lesson on how to accomplish this. In short, define those areas where you will allow your child to push back and negotiate a different outcome, but only do this for preplanned situations and requiring your child to modify their alternative idea.

7. At a restaurant for a ten-year-old you may say, "I want you to order the fish, but you can order something else, as long as it is from the seafood section."

8. Register your child in an activity or sport that makes winning a priority. You can have them engage in other non-competitive activities as well, but in certain situations, set the stage for winning or losing. Winning does matter in many situations or life experiences, always have your child involved in some form of activity that has as its goal a win.

15

Are you a wimp, or do you Parent with Courage?

ANSWER THE FOLLOWING ten questions to see if you Parent with Courage. Encourage others that are involved in the parenting of your child, grandparents, uncles, aunts, or your partner to also complete the survey. How do you rate? How do they rate?

At the end of the survey you will see the implications of your score and my thoughts on what it may mean. If you choose to work and use the strategies I've discussed in this book, take the survey again after about two to three months of work. It will take some time, but with effort you will begin to Parent with Courage and raise a strong leader.

The Parenting with Courage Checklist

1. What is the level of discipline and structure in your home?

   None 0-1-2-3-4-5-6-7-8-9-10 Very much.

2. How often do you say "no" to your child?

   Never 0-1-2-3-4-5-6-7-8-9-10 Often

3. Do you spend one-on-one time with your child for at least thirty minutes each week?

   Never 0-1-2-3-4-5-6-7-8-9-10 Most of the Time

4. You have a strong work ethic and demonstrate this to your child.

   Never 0-1-2-3-4-5-6-7-8-9-10 Very much

5. You believe that children should begin working at an early age and require that your child do so.

   Not at All 0-1-2-3-4-5-6-7-8-9-10 All of the Time

6. You believe that, on occasion, punishing your child is part of the parenting job, and you are able to do this.

   Not at all 0-1-2-3-4-5-6-7-8-9-10 Very Much

7. You accept that oppositional behaviour is necessary for strong leadership, but work to modify, not eliminate, it in your child.

   Not at all 0-1-2-3-4-5-6-7-8-9-10 Very Much

8. You place your child in competitive situations that have only one winner.

   Never 0-1-2-3-4-5-6-7-8-9-10 Very Often

9. You believe that strong boundaries are necessary and that you are not your child's best friend.

   Not at All 0-1-2-3-4-5-6-7-8-9-10 All the time

10. There are many decisions for your child at an early age and even a few when they are eighteen years of age that you make without discussion or negotiation with them.

    Never 0-1-2-3-4-5-6-7-8-9-10 Always

    Now add up your score:_____

Score of 80-100: Congratulations, you are making those tough decisions and are parenting with courage.

Score of 60-79: You could use some parent confidence building. You are doing many good things; let's make you stronger.

Score of 50-60: Who's in charge at home? There is a risk that your children will be controlling your house and life shortly.

Less than 50: Perhaps you feel that genetics, environment, or random chance will make up for your lack of parental courage. It's never too late to change this, regardless of your child's age. The question is, are you ready to make the changes necessary and get started today?

Appendix 1

SPANKING IN CANADA

Here is the legal documentation from the Government of Canada Web Site. Very shortly the government is suggesting to table a bill to override a Supreme Court Decision and make spanking illegal in Canada. At the writing of this book, the following guidelines continue to be law. Keep in mind that despite this decision, the Children Protection Agency or Child Welfare Office where you live may decide to investigate all incidents of spanking as suspected abuse regardless of the context.

http://www.lop.parl.gc.ca/content/lop/researchpublications/prb0510-e.htm

INTRODUCTION

Section 43 of the *Criminal Code* is controversial in that it expressly offers parents and teachers a defence when they use reasonable force to discipline a child. Given an increased recognition of the rights and best interests of children, many have called for an end to any form of physical punishment of children and youth in Canada, which would necessarily include the repeal of s. 43. Others, while acknowledging that abuse itself is never justified, have argued that minor physical correction is acceptable in certain circumstances and that individuals should not risk criminal prosecution as a result of their parenting techniques.

This paper reviews the content of s. 43 and its relatively recent judicial interpretation by the Supreme Court of Canada, a majority of which upheld the provision in 2004. It then discusses past proposals to repeal the section, and the legal effects that such a repeal would have, given the definition of assault in Canada's *Criminal Code* and the availability of common law defences. Finally, public opinion on abolishing s. 43, research regarding the effects of physical punishment and international perspectives on the issue are briefly examined.

SECTION 43 OF THE CRIMINAL CODE

Section 43 of the *Criminal Code*(1) reads as follows:

Every schoolteacher, parent or person standing in the

place of a parent is justified in using force by way of correction toward a pupil or child, as the case may be, who is under his care, if the force does not exceed what is reasonable under the circumstances.

The defence of reasonable correction appeared in Canada's first *Criminal Code* in 1892. The content has remained virtually unchanged since that time, with the exception of the removal of masters and apprentices from among the relationships covered by the defence.(2)

CANADIAN FOUNDATION FOR CHILDREN, YOUTH AND THE LAW V. CANADA (ATTORNEY GENERAL)

On 30 January 2004, the Supreme Court of Canada released its decision in the case of *Canadian Foundation for Children, Youth and the Law* v. *Canada (Attorney General)*.(3) The issue was whether s. 43 is unconstitutional. Six of nine justices concluded that the provision does not violate the *Canadian Charter of Rights and Freedoms*,(4) as it does not infringe a child's rights to security of the person or a child's right to equality, and it does not constitute cruel and unusual treatment or punishment. Three justices dissented in three different respects.

A. Opinion of the Majority

The majority of justices in *Canadian Foundation for Children, Youth and the Law* upheld s. 43 on the basis that it protects only parents, schoolteachers and persons who have assumed all of the obligations of parent-

183

hood. Further, it maintains a risk of criminal sanction if force is used for non-educative or non-corrective purposes, and limits the type and degree of force that may be used. The words "by way of correction" in s. 43 mean that the use of force must be sober and reasoned, address actual behaviour, and be intended to restrain, control, or express symbolic disapproval. The child must have the capacity to understand and benefit from the correction, so that s. 43 does not justify force against children under two or those with particular disabilities.

The words "reasonable under the circumstances" in s. 43 mean that the force must be transitory and trifling, must not harm or degrade the child, and must not be based on the gravity of the wrongdoing. Reasonableness further implies that force may not be administered to teenagers, as it can induce aggressive or antisocial behaviour, may not involve objects such as rulers or belts, and may not be applied to the head. While corporal punishment itself is not reasonable in the school context, a majority of the Supreme Court concluded that teachers may use force to remove children from classrooms or secure compliance with instructions.

B. Dissenting Opinions

In a first dissenting opinion, Binnie J. concluded that s. 43 violates children's equality under s. 15 of the Charter. However, the infringement is justified under s. 1 as reasonable in a free and democratic society, although only with respect to parents and persons standing in their place. Because the justification rests on respecting the family environment where only limited corrective force is used to carry out important parental responsibilities, Binnie J. concluded that the defence in s. 43 should not be available to teachers.

Arbour J., also dissenting, found s. 43 unconstitutionally vague and therefore a violation of children's security that is not in accordance with fundamental principles of justice under s. 7 of the Charter. Citing a lack of judicial consensus on what constitutes force that is "reasonable under the circumstances," she found s. 43 to be incapable of providing clear guidance to parents, teachers and law enforcers.

In a third dissenting opinion, Deschamps J. determined that s. 43 violates s. 15 of the Charter because it "encourages a view of children as less worthy of protection and respect for their bodily integrity based on outdated notions of their inferior personhood."(5) Although reasonable flexibility in child-rearing is a valid objective, a law that permits more than only very minor applications of force unjustifiably impairs the rights of children. Deschamps J. would therefore have struck down s. 43 for both parents and teachers.

PROPOSALS FOR REFORM

In 1984, the Law Reform Commission of Canada recommended the repeal of s. 43 as a defence for teachers. (6) A majority of the Commission suggested that s. 43 be maintained for parents, primarily out of concern that the criminal law would otherwise unduly encroach on family life for every trivial slap or spanking.(7)

There have been several legislative attempts to abolish corporal punishment over the past decade, all in the form of private members' bills introduced in the Senate or House of Commons.(8) The most recent one was introduced in the Senate in October 2007 and received third reading in June 2008. The bill received first reading in the House of Commons on 20 June 2008.(9)

LEGAL EFFECTS OF A REPEAL OF SECTION 43

A. Application of Other Criminal Code Provisions

If s. 43 were repealed, the general assault provisions of the *Criminal Code* would apply to a parent, teacher, or guardian who uses force against a child without the latter's consent. A statutory defence based on "reasonable correction" would no longer be available. Because s. 265 of the *Criminal Code* prohibits the non-consensual application of force and s. 279 prohibits forcible confinement of another person without lawful authority, there is concern that the abolition of the defence in s. 43 would criminalize parental conduct short of what is usually considered corporal punishment, such as restraining an uncooperative child in a car seat or physically putting a child to bed.

Possible responses are that such actions could be defended

under common law doctrines, which are discussed below, or on the basis of a child's implied consent to allow a parent to care for and nurture him or her. Alternatively, law enforcers may, in practice, exercise discretion not to prosecute. Comparisons might be made to various types of unwanted contact between adults that legally constitute assault but are addressed through other measures, such as public education and workplace policies, or not addressed at all. Varying degrees of culpability, depending on the severity of the physical force used, may also be addressed through sentencing.

B. Resort to Common Law Defences

If the defence of reasonable correction in s. 43 were repealed, common law defences would remain.(10) The common law defence of necessity precludes criminal responsibility in emergency situations for involuntary conduct aimed at protecting oneself or others. As it is based on true involuntariness of an action, the defence has been interpreted narrowly.(11) Three elements must be present: imminent peril or danger, the absence of a reasonable legal alternative, and proportionality between the harm inflicted and the harm avoided. While the defence might be available, for example, to a parent preventing a child from running into the street, it would not be available to a parent who, with or without thinking, strikes a child who is misbehaving.

The defence of *de minimus*(12) is an alternative common law defence that precludes punishment for a trivial or technical violation of the law. Compared to that of necessity, this defence is more likely to relieve parents and guardians of criminal convictions resulting from minor forms of physical punishment. However, it may not be as available to teachers, given society's growing lack of acceptance of the use of corporal punishment in schools. The *de minimus* defence depends on whether the offence may be viewed as not serious, and the offender not deserving of criminal sanction.

C. Provincial Laws

Under their legislative authority over education and child protection, some provinces and territories have already prohibited corporal punishment in schools and childcare facilities.(13) Quebec removed references to a "right of correction" from its *Civil Code* in 1994.(14) However, legislation is inconsistent across the country. Should Parliament repeal s. 43 under its criminal law power, physical punishment of children would become unlawful in all Canadian jurisdictions. Any provincial or territorial law that remained inconsistent would yield to the paramount federal statute. The repeal of s. 43 would therefore create legal consistency across Canada.

Public Opinion and Social Science Research

The issue of whether parents should be permitted to use physical punishment on their children is divisive in Canada. A national survey in 2003(15) indicated that a large majority (69%) of Canadians were in favour of repealing s. 43 of the *Criminal Code* with respect to teachers. However, this majority was less supportive (51%) with respect to ending the provision for parents. The same survey found that respondents were more inclined to support the removal of s. 43 if guidelines were developed to prevent prosecutions of minor slaps or spanks (60%), research demonstrated that physical punishment is ineffective and potentially harmful (61%), or research showed that ending s. 43 would decrease abuse (71%).

Over 100 organizations and individuals in Canada have endorsed a position stating that physical punishment of children and youth plays no useful role in their upbringing, and calling for the same protection from assault as that given to Canadian adults.(16) Other groups, conversely, support the parental protection offered by s. 43 and argue that parents should be free to decide how to discipline their children, provided that it is fair, reasonable and never abusive.(17)

There is a growing body of research indicating that corporal punishment has detrimental effects on children.(18) It places children at risk of physical injury, physical abuse, impaired mental health, a poor parent/child relationship, and increased childhood and adolescent aggression and antisocial behaviour.(19) However, other researchers dispute these findings. The two main criticisms are that research on the negative effects of corporal punishment does not adequately distinguish between physical punishment and physical abuse, and research cannot determine whether the negative outcomes attributed to physical punishment are actually caused by the punishment.(20)

INTERNATIONAL PERSPECTIVES

In 1991, Canada ratified the United Nations *Convention on the Rights of the Child*, article 19 of which mandates the protection of children from all forms of physical or mental violence, injury or abuse.(21) In response to reports from Canada regarding the action it has taken to meet the requirements of the Convention, the United Nations Committee on the Rights of the Child recommended that physical punishment of children in schools and families be prohibited and that s. 43 be removed. (22) At the same time, international covenants recognize the integrity of the family unit and indicate that parents have the primary responsibility for the upbringing and development of the child.(23) Further, in *Canadian Foundation for Children, Youth and the Law*, a majority of the Supreme Court of Canada considered the *Convention on the Rights of the Child* and concluded that it did not explicitly require state parties to ban all corporal punishment of children.(24)

At least nineteen countries have legislated bans on corporal punishment in both the home and school.(25) Other countries, or jurisdictions within them, have passed laws prohibiting force of certain types or in certain contexts. Although many countries have legislated against corporal punishment, most of the one hundred and ninety-three parties to the *Convention on the Rights of the*

Child have not. Further, those that have, including Sweden, Finland, Denmark, Norway and Austria, have apparently instituted non-criminal measures and reserve assault only for more serious conduct.(26) Because the definition of assault in Canada's *Criminal Code* is based on the non-consensual nature of the contact, there may be greater risk in Canada in extending the criminal law. It may be important to ensure that other defences are available so that parents are not criminally convicted for minor forms of physical punishment.

Conclusion

IN GENERAL, NOBODY disagrees with the proposition that children should be free from physical abuse and injury, and this is clearly not what the debate surrounding s. 43 of the *Criminal Code* is about. Rather, the debate is about the effects of minor forms of physical punishment and the appropriateness of using the criminal law to enforce a particular view of what constitutes proper parenting. Some are confident that prosecutorial discretion and existing common law defences will continue to prevent individuals from being charged or convicted for trivial slaps and spanks. Others fear that parents may face intervention from neighbours or passersby, investigations by police and even imprisonment for limited punishment of their children, or for a momentary, but arguably human, lapse of judgment.

Child welfare and protection laws go some distance in the prevention and detection of child abuse, and public education campaigns exist to encourage parents not to use even minor forms of physical punishment on their children. Given these developments, advocates for the repeal of s. 43 say that the provision sends the mixed message that it may be acceptable to strike a child. But those against the removal of s. 43 from the *Criminal Code* worry about an inverse message: if the provision is repealed, criminal prosecution and conviction may result from any physical contact or restraint that is used against a child. As with most social issues, it is clear that there is no Canadian consensus, which is all the more understandable, given that even the Supreme Court of Canada and the United Nations Committee on the Rights of the Child have expressed divergent views on the acceptability of s. 43.

Endnotes

1. *Criminal Code*, R.S.C. 1985, c. C-46.

2. Section 55 of the 1892 *Criminal Code* read: "It is lawful for every parent, or person in the place of a parent, schoolmaster or master, to use force by way of correction towards any child, pupil or apprentice under his care, provided that such force is reasonable under the circumstances."

3. *Canadian Foundation for Children, Youth and the Law* v. *Canada (Attorney General)*, 2004 SCC 4, aff'g (2002), 57 O.R. (3d) 511 (C.A.), aff'g (2000), 49 O.R. (3d) 662 (S.C.) ["*CFCYL v. Canada*"].

4. *Canadian Charter of Rights and Freedoms*, Part 1 of the *Constitution Act, 1982*, being Schedule B to the *Canada*

Act 1982 (U.K.), 1982, c. 11, s. 7 (security of the person), s. 12 (cruel and unusual punishment), and s. 15 (equality).

5. *CFCYL* v. *Canada*, para. 232.

6. Law Reform Commission of Canada, *Assault*, Working Paper 38, Ministry of Supply and Services, Ottawa, 1984, pp. 44 and 53.

7. *Ibid.*, pp. 44-45 and 53.

8. See, e.g., An Act to amend the Criminal Code (protection of children), Bill C-305, 2nd Session, 35th Parliament, 1996 (MP Robinson); An Act to amend the Criminal Code and the Department of Health Act (security of the child), Bill S-14, 2nd Session, 35th Parliament, 1996 (Sen. Carstairs); An Act to amend the Criminal Code (protection of children), Bill C-276, 1st Session, 36th Parliament, 1997 (MP Davies); An Act to amend the Criminal Code and the Department of Health Act (security of the child), Bill C-368, 1st Session, 36th Parliament, 1998 (MP Ianno); An Act to amend the Criminal Code (protection of children), Bill C-329, 1st Session, 37th Parliament, 2001 (MP Davies); An Act to amend the Criminal Code (protection of children), Bill S-21, 1st Session, 38th Parliament, 2004 (Sen. Hervieux-Payette); An Act to amend the Criminal Code (protection of children), Bill S-207, 1st Session, 39th Parliament, 2006 (Sen. Hervieux-Payette).

9. An Act to amend the Criminal Code (protection of children), Bill S-209, 2nd Session, 39th Parliament, 2006 (Sen. Hervieux-Payette).

10. Common law defences are expressly available by virtue of s. 8(3) of the *Criminal Code*. Certain statutory defences, though limited in scope, would also remain available, such as those permitting no more force than is necessary to protect oneself (e.g., ss. 34, 35 and 37), to protect others (e.g., s. 37), or to protect property (e.g., s. 39).

11. See, e.g., *R.* v. *Perka*, [1984] 2 S.C.R. 232, 13 D.L.R. (4th) 1 and *R.* v. *Latimer*, [2001] 1 S.C.R. 3, 193 D.L.R. (4th) 577.

12. The full maxim is *de minimus non curat lex* and has been stated to mean that the law does not care for small or trifling matters: see Jean Hétu, "De minimus non curat praetor: une maxime qui a toute son importance!" *Revue du Barreau*, Vol. 50, 1990, p. 1065.

13. Physical punishment is prohibited under legislation governing day cares in British Columbia, Alberta, Saskatchewan, Manitoba, Ontario, Nova Scotia, Prince Edward Island, Newfoundland and Labrador, Yukon, Northwest Territories and Nunavut and under legislation governing schools and education in British Columbia, Quebec, New Brunswick, Nova Scotia, Prince Edward Island, Newfoundland and Labrador, Yukon, Northwest Territories and Nunavut: see Nico Trocmé *et al.*, *Physical abuse of children in the context of punishment*, Centre of Excellence for Child Welfare, Information Sheet #8E, Ottawa, 2003.

14. Reasonable and moderate correction was permitted under art. 651 of the *Civil Code of Quebec* (1980) (*An Act to*

establish a new Civil Code and to reform family law), S.Q. 1980, c. 39, but did not reappear in the *Civil Code of Quebec* (1994), S.Q. 1991, c. 64. Opinion differs as to whether a right of correction, ancillary to the rights of custody, supervision and education, remains in Quebec's general law: see Claire Bernard, "Corporal Punishment as a Means of Correcting Children," Commission des droits de la personne et des droits de la jeunesse, Québec, November 1998.

15. Toronto Public Health, National Survey of Canadians' Attitudes on Section 43 of the Criminal Code, September 2003.

16. Joan Durrant, Ron Ensom and Coalition on Physical Punishment of Children and Youth, *Joint Statement on Physical Punishment of Children and Youth*, Ottawa, September 2004 and March 2005.

17. E.g., Coalition for Family Autonomy and REAL Women of Canada.

18. See, e.g., Elizabeth Gershoff, "Corporal Punishment by Parents and Associated Child Behaviors and Experiences: A Meta-Analytic and Theoretical Review," *Psychological Bulletin*, Vol. 128, No. 4, 2002. See also Murray A. Straus, David Sugarman and Jean Giles-Sims, "Spanking by Parents and Subsequent Antisocial Behavior of Children," *Archives of Pediatrics and Adolescent Medicine*, Vol. 151, No. 8, August 1997.

19. See, e.g., Joan Durrant and Ron Ensom, *Physical punishment of children*, Centre of Excellence for Child Welfare, Information Sheet #7E, Ottawa, 2004.

20. See, e.g., Robert E. Larzelere and Brett R. Kuhn, "Comparing Child Outcomes of Physical Punishment and Alternative Disciplinary Tactics: A Meta-Analysis," *Clinical Child and Family Psychology Review*, Vol. 8, No. 1, March 2005. See also Diana Baumrind, "Does Causally Relevant Research Support a Blanket Injunction Against Disciplinary Spanking by Parents?" Invited Address at the 109th Annual Convention of the American Psychological Association, San Francisco, August 2001.

21. *Convention on the Rights of the Child*, 20 November 1989, CAN. T.S. 1992 No. 3, art. 19(1): "States Parties shall take all appropriate legislative, administrative, social and educational measures to protect the child from all forms of physical or mental violence, injury or abuse, neglect or negligent treatment, maltreatment or exploitation, including sexual abuse, while in the care of parent(s), legal guardian(s) or any other person who has the care of the child."

22. United Nations Committee on the Rights of the Child, Consideration of Reports Submitted by States Parties under Article 44 of the Convention, Concluding Observations of the Committee on the Rights of the Child: Canada, CRC/C/15/Add.37, 20 June 1995, paras. 14 and 25, and CRC/C/15/Add.215, 27 October 2003, para. 32. In response to Canada's second report, the Committee stated that "it is deeply concerned that the State party has not enacted legislation explicitly prohibiting all forms of corporal punishment and has

taken no action to remove section 43 of the Criminal Code, which allows corporal punishment."

23. *International Covenant on Civil and Political Rights*, 16 December 1966, Can. T.S. 1976 No. 47, art. 23(1): "The family is the natural and fundamental group unit of society and is entitled to protection by society and the State." *International Covenant on Economic, Social and Cultural Rights*, 16 December 1966, Can. T.S. 1976 No. 46, art. 10(1): "The widest possible protection and assistance should be accorded to the family, which is the natural and fundamental group unit of society, particularly for its establishment and while it is responsible for the care and education of dependent children." *Convention on the Rights of the Child*, art. 18(1): "Parents or, as the case may be, legal guardians, have the primary responsibility for the upbringing and development of the child."

24. *CFCYL* v. *Canada*, para. 33.

25. Austria, Bulgaria, Croatia, Cyprus, Denmark, Finland, Germany, Greece, Hungary, Israel, Iceland, Latvia, New Zealand, Netherlands, Norway, Portugal, Romania, Sweden and the Ukraine. Source: Global Initiative to End All Corporal Punishment of Children, London, U.K.

26. Sweden, for example, has legislated against physical punishment of children in its *Code of Parental Responsibilities*: see Adamira Tijerino, "Under Scrutiny: Corporal Punishment and Section 43 of the Criminal Code of Canada," Draft Document, B.C. Institute Against Family Violence, Vancouver, 2001 (section V).

77308186R00115

Made in the USA
Middletown, DE
20 June 2018